Prayer Journal for

Catholic
Moms

Prayer Journal for

Catholic Moms

A 52-week Guided Devotional
with Scripture, the Saints, and fellow Christians
towards Peace, Purpose, and Clarity

Compiled and Written by

Mary Nadeau Reed

Edited by and Adapted from
Scott L. Smith, Jr.

HOLYWATERBOOKS

Prayer Journal for Catholic Moms: A 52-week Guided Devotional with Scripture, the Saints, and fellow Christians towards Peace, Purpose, and Clarity

Copyright © 2023 Mary Nadeau Reed; Scott L. Smith, Jr., editor

Paperback ISBN-13: 978-1-950782-55-0
Hardcover ISBN-13: 978-1-950782-56-7
All rights reserved.
Holy Water Books (Publisher)

HOLYWATERBOOKS

please check out our
other titles online at
www.holywaterbooks.com

Unless otherwise noted, all quotes from Scripture included in this book are from the Revised Standard Version – Catholic Edition (RSV-CE), and all quotes from Sarah MacKenzie are from her book *Teaching from Rest*.

"Pray, hope, and don' t worry.
Worry is useless.
God is merciful and will hear your prayer."

St. (Padre) Pio of Pietrelcina

Table of Contents

Foreword

Dear friend, we hope that this journal will provide a space for you to be nurtured and filled, so that you can better bring life and joy to your family! We pray you encounter the Lord in these pages, and draw closer to His heart.

Though this journal is designed for 52 weeks of guided prayer, it could be used in numerous other ways. You could use it for a continuous 52 day retreat, or work your way through it at any other pace. You can go through all the components for the week in one day, or divide them for prayer throughout your week. You can also utilize this text as a more traditional prayer book, looking up prayers specific to your present circumstances in the table of contents. All that matters is that you are using it in the way that enriches your prayer life, so that you may feel refreshed and equipped in your vocation.

Each of the 52 weeks (or days, if you prefer) includes a seven-step prayer sequence modeled after the *Examen* prayer of St. Ignatius:

1. The first step, **Breathe**, guides us through a breathing exercise. Such exercises are commonly used to work through occasions of anxiety or stress, and can be a great resource at other times during your day.
    Note: If the number of seconds of breathing in and out don't work well for you physically, feel free to alter the protocol, e.g. breathing in for 5 seconds instead of 7.

2. We take time to become aware of **God's presence**. We remember that He is closer to us than we are to ourselves. With us right now, in the now. As St. Augustine says, "Our hearts were made for You, O Lord, and they are restless until they rest in You."

3. **Thanksgiving** is key to finding peace and purpose, and overcoming daily stressors. We reorient ourselves to gratitude, focusing less on our fears and more on God's gifts.

4. We **Reflect** on a Scripture verse and a quote of a saint, fellow Christian, or other insightful individual. We chose these quotes and verses specifically to help gain perspective and peace as we engage in our vocations. When reading the scripture verse, we consider what words stand out to us. Ask yourself what comes into your mind or how do you feel as you reflect on the words, and speak to the Lord about those feelings and thoughts. This is the meditative practice of lectio divina. We sit with these passages for five minutes or more, rereading slower each time, observing which words stand out to us. We plant these words in our minds, water them daily with reflection, and let them take root.

5. We ask the Lord to guide our reflection upon our day and week. Jesus takes us by the hand to **Examine** the moments and experiences of our lives. We wait and

see what bubbles up in our memories. What is Jesus trying to reveal to us? He may show us the way He was present in our moments, even if we did not see Him there. Over time, this exercise helps us have confidence that Jesus never leaves our sides; to sense His constant presence.

6. We embrace **Contrition**. We consider the ways that sin creeped into our day, the ways we did not love as we should have. Recognizing our own triggers, temptations, and patterns can be a wonderful opportunity for us to refashion our habits into virtues. We express our trust and gratitude for God's mercy, and ask for grace to transform our habits.

7. We learn to prayerfully anticipate the future in **Hope**, expressing our firm trust that God is working all things out for our ultimate good.

Every week we consider a different **Weekly Prayer** either from the wealth of Catholic tradition, or composed specifically for this journal. We also have an opportunity to consider our:

- **Prayer Intentions:** This is an opportunity to give everything to the Lord. Journaling the things that occupy our heart helps us to leave them in Jesus' outstretched hands. We can pray for loved ones, and for those people who have caused us or a loved one sorrow. This is an amazing way to find healing and freedom.

- **Goals Checklist:** Modify this list as needed. It helps us to track our progress in entering more deeply into the sacramental life of the church.

- **Small Things with Great Love:** We take note of times that we recently engaged in an act of charity or courage. When we went above and beyond, or simply did what we had to, but with joy. By journaling these acts of love and sacrifice, we make these acts a more overt gift to the Lord, and we can be better aware of opportunities to do so in the future.

We hope you allow this journal to serve you. That you utilize the aspects that expand your heart and give you peace. Disregard anything that does not. Be assured of our prayers for you as you endeavor to nurture truth, goodness, and beauty within your family. *Ad majórem Dei glóriam!* (For the greater glory of God!)

In Christ,

Mary Nadeau Reed

Prayer Journal for
Catholic Moms

first, Breathe

Breathe in ...
7 seconds.
Hold your breath ...
7 seconds.
Breathe out ...
7 seconds.

Repeat.

As many times
as you like.

second, Become aware of God's Presence

third, Thanksgiving

Lord, I realize that all, even myself, is a gift from you. Today, for what things am I most grateful?

fourth, Reflect

Psalm 143:8

"Let go of your plans. The first hour of your morning belongs to God. Tackle the day's work that he charges you with, and he will give you the power to accomplish it." – St. Edith Stein

fifth, Examination

Lord, open my eyes and ears to be more honest with myself. Show me what has been happening to me and in me this day. Today, how have I experienced your love?

_____
_____
_____
_____
_____
_____
_____
_____
_____
_____

sixth Contrition

Today, what choices have been inadequate responses to your love?

_____
_____
_____
_____
_____
_____

seventh, Hope

Lord, let me look with longing toward the future. How will I let you lead me to a brighter tomorrow?

_____
_____
_____
_____
_____
_____

Weekly
Prayer

Prayer of Abandonment
by Charles de Foucauld

Father,
I abandon myself into your hands;
do with me what you will.
Whatever you may do, I thank you:
I am ready for all, I accept all.
Let only your will be done in me,
and in all your creatures –
I wish no more than this, O Lord.
Into your hands I commend my soul:
I offer it to you with all the love of my heart,
for I love you, Lord, and so need to give myself,
to surrender myself into your hands without
reserve,
and with boundless confidence,
for you are my Father.
Amen.

Prayer Goals

Prayer Intentions

For whom or what do I want to pray this week? Anyone who frustrates me, or has caused harm to myself or those I love. Anyone/anything who has touched my heart.

_____
_____
_____
_____
_____
_____
_____
_____
_____
_____

"Not all of us can do great things. But we can do *small things with great love.*"
—Mother Teresa of Calcutta

My "small things" this week:

_____
_____
_____
_____
_____
_____
_____
_____
_____
_____
_____
_____
_____

Checklist

We draw a box next to any goals we want to make for ourselves this week, and check them off as we go.

Morning Offering

Evening Prayer or Liturgy of the Hours

Daily/Weekly Rosary

Angelus

Scripture Reading

Divine Mercy Chaplet

Other: _____

Weekday/Daily Mass

Confession

Fasting

Read a Saint Biography

Give alms or a donation

Novena

Volunteer at Homeless Shelter or Food Bank
(or other Corporal Work of Mercy)

first,
Breathe

Breathe in ...
7 seconds.
Hold your breath ...
7 seconds.
Breathe out ...
7 seconds.

Repeat.

As many times
as you like.

second,
Become aware of
God's Presence

third,
Thanksgiving

Lord, I realize that all, even myself, is a gift from you. Today, for what things am I most grateful?

fourth, Reflect

Proverbs 31:31

""Take care of your body as if you were going to live forever, and take care of your soul as if you were going to die tomorrow."
-St. Augustine

fifth, Examination

Lord, open my eyes and ears to be more honest with myself. Show me what has been happening to me and in me this day. Today, how have I experienced your love?

_____
_____
_____
_____
_____
_____
_____
_____
_____

sixth Contrition

Today, what choices have been inadequate responses to your love?

_____
_____
_____
_____
_____
_____

seventh, Hope

Lord, let me look with longing toward the future. How will I let you lead me to a brighter tomorrow?

_____
_____
_____
_____
_____
_____

Weekly
Prayer

Prayer for the Strength to Care for Myself
by Mary Nadeau Reed

Dear Lord,
So many things need doing.
So many people need loving.
My needs, my desires, my heart,
They can seem like luxuries my schedule can't afford.
But my children are watching me.
My daughters are observing,
Deciding if they feel called to this vocation.
My sons, they see me.
They draw conclusions about
what their wives' needs will be one day.
I am the one who shows them how a woman of God
gives You glory in herself.
Give me peace and strength in caring for Your daughter,
for myself.
In enriching and nurturing the soil of my heart,
So that I can give my family an even richer harvest.
And when all else fails,
and there aren't enough hours in the day,
Give me the peace of knowing I'm Your beloved daughter.
To You be all glory and honor.
Amen.

Prayer Goals

Prayer Intentions

For whom or what do I want to pray this week? Anyone who frustrates me, or has caused harm to myself or those I love. Anyone/anything who has touched my heart.

_____
_____
_____
_____
_____
_____
_____
_____
_____
_____
_____

> "Not all of us can do great things. But we can do
> **small things with great love."**
> -Mother Teresa of Calcutta

My "small things" this week:

_____
_____
_____
_____
_____
_____
_____
_____
_____
_____
_____
_____

Checklist

We draw a box next to any goals we want to make for ourselves this week, and check them off as we go.

Morning Offering

Evening Prayer or Liturgy of the Hours

Daily/Weekly Rosary

Angelus

Scripture Reading

Divine Mercy Chaplet

Other: _____

Weekday/Daily Mass

Confession

Fasting

Read a Saint Biography

Give alms or a donation

Novena

Volunteer at Homeless Shelter or Food Bank
(or other Corporal Work of Mercy)

first, Breathe

Breathe in ...
7 seconds.
Hold your breath ...
7 seconds.
Breathe out ...
7 seconds.

Repeat.

As many times
as you like.

second, Become aware of God's Presence

third, Thanksgiving

Lord, I realize that all, even myself, is a gift from you. Today, for what things am I most grateful?

fourth, *Reflect*

Deuteronomy 4:9

"Remember that the gift of grace increases as the struggle increases."
– St. Rose of Lima

fifth, *Examination*

Lord, open my eyes and ears to be more honest with myself. Show me what has been happening to me and in me this day. Today, how have I experienced your love?

_____   _____
_____   _____
_____   _____
_____   _____
_____   _____
_____   _____
_____   _____
_____   _____

sixth *Contrition*

Today, what choices have been inadequate responses to your love?

_____
_____
_____
_____
_____
_____

seventh, *Hope*

Lord, let me look with longing toward the future. How will I let you lead me to a brighter tomorrow?

_____
_____
_____
_____
_____
_____

Weekly
Prayer

Prayer of
Saint Richard of Chichester

Thanks be to thee,
My Lord Jesus Christ,
For all the benefits Thou hast given me,
For all the pains and insults
Thou hast borne for me.
O most merciful redeemer,
Friend and Brother,
May I know Thee more clearly,
Love Thee more dearly, and
Follow Thee more nearly,
Day by day.
Amen.

Prayer Goals

Prayer Intentions

For whom or what do I want to pray this week? Anyone who frustrates me, or has caused harm to myself or those I love. Anyone/anything who has touched my heart.

_____
_____
_____
_____
_____
_____
_____
_____

"Not all of us can do great things. But we can do

small things with great love."

-Mother Teresa of Calcutta

My "small things" this week:

_____
_____
_____
_____
_____
_____
_____
_____
_____
_____
_____
_____

Checklist

We draw a box next to any goals we want to make for ourselves this week, and check them off as we go.

Morning Offering

Evening Prayer or Liturgy of the Hours

Daily/Weekly Rosary

Angelus

Scripture Reading

Divine Mercy Chaplet

Other: _____

Weekday/Daily Mass

Confession

Fasting

Read a Saint Biography

Give alms or a donation

Novena

Volunteer at Homeless Shelter or Food Bank
(or other Corporal Work of Mercy)

first, Breathe

Breathe in ...
7 seconds.
Hold your breath ...
7 seconds.
Breathe out ...
7 seconds.

Repeat.

As many times
as you like.

second, Become aware of God's Presence

third, Thanksgiving

Lord, I realize that all, even myself, is a gift from you. Today, for what things am I most grateful?

fourth,
Reflect

1 John 4:19

"When I try, I fail. When I trust, He succeeds."
-Corrie Ten Boom (Concentration Camp Survivor, Christian Writer/Speaker)

fifth, Examination

Lord, open my eyes and ears to be more honest with myself. Show me what has been happening to me and in me this day. Today, how have I experienced your love?

_____
_____
_____
_____
_____
_____
_____
_____
_____
_____
_____
_____
_____
_____

sixth Contrition

Today, what choices have been inadequate responses to your love?

_____
_____
_____
_____
_____
_____
_____
_____

seventh, Hope

Lord, let me look with longing toward the future. How will I let you lead me to a brighter tomorrow?

_____
_____
_____
_____
_____
_____
_____
_____

Weekly
Prayer

Act of Abandonment of St. Francis de Sales

O my God, I thank You and I praise
You for accomplishing Your holy
and all-lovable will without any regard for mine.
With my whole heart,
in spite of my heart,
do I receive this cross I feared so much!

It is the cross of Your choice,
the cross of Your love.
I venerate it;
nor for anything in the world
would I wish that it had not come,
since You willed it.

I keep it with gratitude and with joy,
as I do everything that comes from Your hand;
and I shall strive to carry it without letting it drag,
with all the respect
and all the affection which Your works deserve.
Amen.

Prayer Goals

Prayer Intentions

For whom or what do I want to pray this week? Anyone who frustrates me, or has caused harm to myself or those I love. Anyone/anything who has touched my heart.

_____
_____
_____
_____
_____
_____
_____
_____
_____
_____
_____

> "Not all of us can do great things. But we can do _small things with great love._"
> —Mother Teresa of Calcutta

My "small things" this week:

_____
_____
_____
_____
_____
_____
_____
_____
_____
_____
_____
_____

Checklist

We draw a box next to any goals we want to make for ourselves this week, and check them off as we go.

Morning Offering

Evening Prayer or Liturgy of the Hours

Daily/Weekly Rosary

Angelus

Scripture Reading

Divine Mercy Chaplet

Other: _____

Weekday/Daily Mass

Confession

Fasting

Read a Saint Biography

Give alms or a donation

Novena

Volunteer at Homeless Shelter or Food Bank
(or other Corporal Work of Mercy)

first, Breathe

Breathe in ...
7 seconds.
Hold your breath ...
7 seconds.
Breathe out ...
7 seconds.

Repeat.

As many times
as you like.

second, Become aware of God's Presence

third, Thanksgiving

Lord, I realize that all, even myself, is a gift from you. Today, for what things am I most grateful?

fourth,
Reflect

Proverbs 22:6

"(The formation and education of children) is not the filling of a pail, but the lighting of a fire." – William Butler Yeats

fifth,
Examination

Lord, open my eyes and ears to be more honest with myself. Show me what has been happening to me and in me this day. Today, how have I experienced your love?

_____
_____
_____
_____
_____
_____
_____
_____
_____
_____
_____

sixth,
Contrition

Today, what choices have been inadequate responses to your love?

_____
_____
_____
_____
_____
_____

seventh,
Hope

Lord, let me look with longing toward the future. How will I let you lead me to a brighter tomorrow?

_____
_____
_____
_____
_____
_____

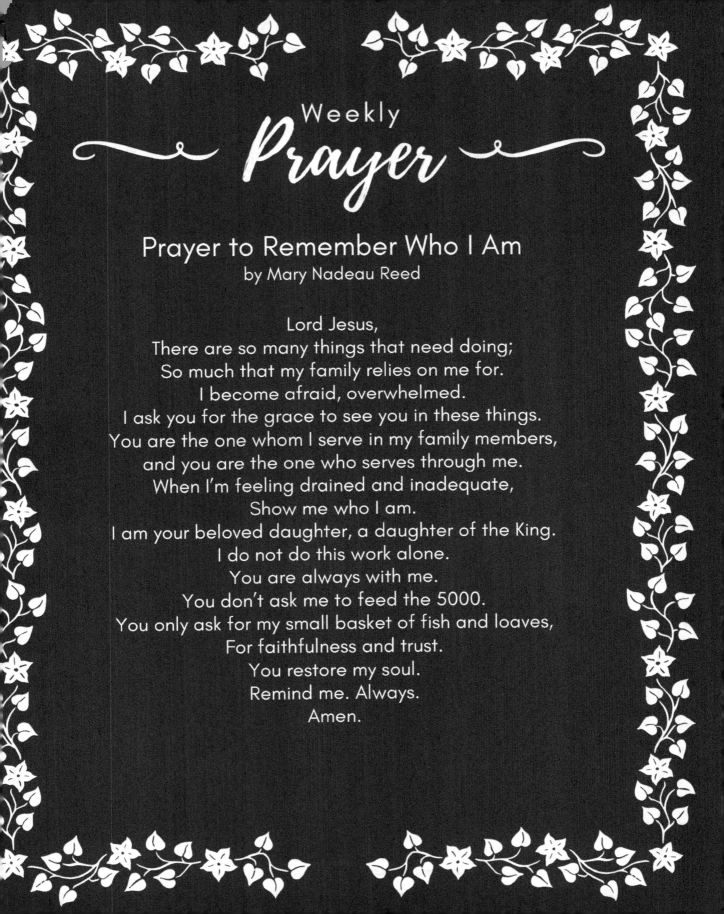

Weekly
Prayer

Prayer to Remember Who I Am
by Mary Nadeau Reed

Lord Jesus,
There are so many things that need doing;
So much that my family relies on me for.
I become afraid, overwhelmed.
I ask you for the grace to see you in these things.
You are the one whom I serve in my family members,
and you are the one who serves through me.
When I'm feeling drained and inadequate,
Show me who I am.
I am your beloved daughter, a daughter of the King.
I do not do this work alone.
You are always with me.
You don't ask me to feed the 5000.
You only ask for my small basket of fish and loaves,
For faithfulness and trust.
You restore my soul.
Remind me. Always.
Amen.

Prayer Goals

Prayer Intentions

For whom or what do I want to pray this week? Anyone who frustrates me, or has caused harm to myself or those I love. Anyone/anything who has touched my heart.

_____
_____
_____
_____
_____
_____
_____

"Not all of us can do great things. But we can do _small things with great love._"
-Mother Teresa of Calcutta

My "small things" this week:

_____
_____
_____
_____
_____
_____
_____
_____
_____
_____
_____

Checklist

We draw a box next to any goals we want to make for ourselves this week, and check them off as we go.

Morning Offering

Evening Prayer or Liturgy of the Hours

Daily/Weekly Rosary

Angelus

Scripture Reading

Divine Mercy Chaplet

Other: _____

Weekday/Daily Mass

Confession

Fasting

Read a Saint Biography

Give alms or a donation

Novena

Volunteer at Homeless Shelter or Food Bank
(or other Corporal Work of Mercy)

first, Breathe

Breathe in ...
7 seconds.
Hold your breath ...
7 seconds.
Breathe out ...
7 seconds.

Repeat.

As many times
as you like.

second, Become aware of God's Presence

third, Thanksgiving

Lord, I realize that all, even myself, is a gift from you. Today, for what things am I most grateful?

fourth,
Reflect

Numbers 6:24-26

"Every mother is like Moses. She does not enter the promised land. She prepares a world she will not see."
–Pope Paul VI

fifth, Examination

Lord, open my eyes and ears to be more honest with myself. Show me what has been happening to me and in me this day. Today, how have I experienced your love?

_____
_____
_____
_____
_____
_____
_____
_____
_____
_____
_____
_____

sixth Contrition

Today, what choices have been inadequate responses to your love?

_____
_____
_____
_____
_____
_____
_____
_____

seventh, Hope

Lord, let me look with longing toward the future. How will I let you lead me to a brighter tomorrow?

_____
_____
_____
_____
_____
_____
_____
_____

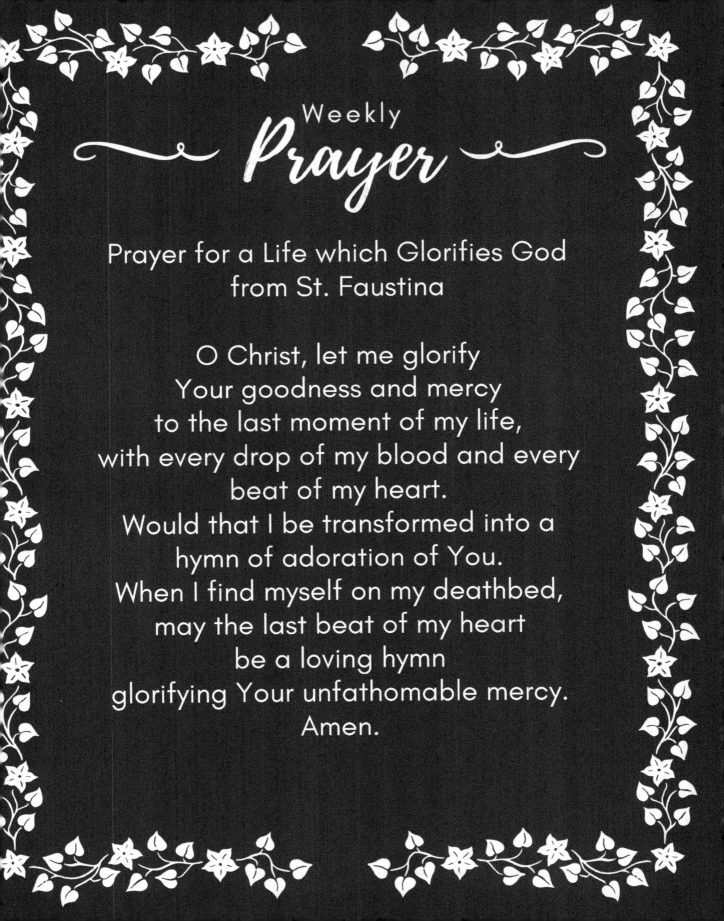

Weekly Prayer

Prayer for a Life which Glorifies God
from St. Faustina

O Christ, let me glorify
Your goodness and mercy
to the last moment of my life,
with every drop of my blood and every
beat of my heart.
Would that I be transformed into a
hymn of adoration of You.
When I find myself on my deathbed,
may the last beat of my heart
be a loving hymn
glorifying Your unfathomable mercy.
Amen.

Prayer Goals

Prayer Intentions

For whom or what do I want to pray this week? Anyone who frustrates me, or has caused harm to myself or those I love. Anyone/anything who has touched my heart.

"Not all of us can do great things. But we can do

small things with great love."

-Mother Teresa of Calcutta

My "small things" this week:

Checklist

We draw a box next to any goals we want to make for ourselves this week, and check them off as we go.

Morning Offering

Evening Prayer or Liturgy of the Hours

Daily/Weekly Rosary

Angelus

Scripture Reading

Divine Mercy Chaplet

Other: _____

Weekday/Daily Mass

Confession

Fasting

Read a Saint Biography

Give alms or a donation

Novena

Volunteer at Homeless Shelter or Food Bank
(or other Corporal Work of Mercy)

first, Breathe

Breathe in ...
7 seconds.
Hold your breath ...
7 seconds.
Breathe out ...
7 seconds.

Repeat.

As many times
as you like.

second, Become aware of God's Presence

third, Thanksgiving

Lord, I realize that all, even myself, is a gift from you. Today, for what things am I most grateful?

fourth,
Reflect

Galatians 5:22-23

"There is no school equal to a decent home
and no teacher equal to a virtuous parent."
-Mahatma Gandhi

fifth,
Examination

Lord, open my eyes and ears to be more honest with myself. Show me what has been happening to me and in me this day. Today, how have I experienced your love?

_____
_____
_____
_____
_____
_____
_____
_____
_____
_____
_____
_____
_____
_____
_____

sixth
Contrition

Today, what choices have been inadequate responses to your love?

_____
_____
_____
_____
_____
_____
_____
_____

seventh,
Hope

Lord, let me look with longing toward the future. How will I let you lead me to a brighter tomorrow?

_____
_____
_____
_____
_____
_____
_____
_____

Weekly
Prayer

Te Deum
Traditionally attributed to St. Ambrose and St. Augustine, 4th Century

O, God, we praise You and acknowledge You
to be the supreme Lord.
Everlasting Father, all the earth worships You.
All the angels, the heavens and all angelic powers,
All the cherubim and seraphim, continually cry to You:
Holy, holy, holy, Lord God of Hosts!
Heaven and earth are full of the majesty of Your glory.
The glorious choir of the apostles,
The wonderful company of prophets,
The white-robed army of martyrs, praise You.
Holy Church throughout the world acknowledges You:
The Father of infinite majesty;
Your adorable, true and only Son;
Also the Holy Spirit, the Comforter.
O Christ, You are the King of glory!
You are the everlasting Son of the Father.
When You took it upon Yourself to deliver man,
You did not disdain the Virgin's womb.
Having overcome the sting of death,
You opened the kingdom of heaven to all believers.
You sit at the right hand of God in the glory of the Father
We believe that You will come to be our Judge.
We, therefore, beg You to help Your servants
whom You have redeemed with Your Precious Blood.
Let them be numbered with Your saints in everlasting glory.
Amen.

Prayer Goals

Prayer Intentions

For whom or what do I want to pray this week? Anyone who frustrates me, or has caused harm to myself or those I love. Anyone/anything who has touched my heart.

"Not all of us can do great things. But we can do *small things with great love.*"
-Mother Teresa of Calcutta

My "small things" this week:

Checklist

We draw a box next to any goals we want to make for ourselves this week, and check them off as we go.

Morning Offering

Evening Prayer or Liturgy of the Hours

Daily/Weekly Rosary

Angelus

Scripture Reading

Divine Mercy Chaplet

Other: _____

Weekday/Daily Mass

Confession

Fasting

Read a Saint Biography

Give alms or a donation

Novena

Volunteer at Homeless Shelter or Food Bank
(or other Corporal Work of Mercy)

first,
Breathe

Breathe in ...
7 seconds.
Hold your breath ...
7 seconds.
Breathe out ...
7 seconds.

Repeat.

As many times
as you like.

second,
Become aware of
God's Presence

third,
Thanksgiving

Lord, I realize that all, even myself, is a gift from you. Today, for what things am I most grateful?

fourth, Reflect

Romans 8:35

"With Jesus, even in our darkest moments the best remains
and the very best is yet to be…"
–Corrie Ten Boom (Concentration Camp Survivor, Christian Writer/Speaker)

fifth, Examination

Lord, open my eyes and ears to be more honest with myself. Show me what has been happening to me and in me this day. Today, how have I experienced your love?

_____

_____

_____

_____

_____

_____

_____

_____

_____

_____

sixth Contrition

Today, what choices have been inadequate responses to your love?

_____

_____

_____

_____

seventh, Hope

Lord, let me look with longing toward the future. How will I let you lead me to a brighter tomorrow?

_____

_____

_____

_____

Weekly
Prayer

A Prayer for Deliverance
from Psalm 25

To Thee, O Lord, I lift up my soul.
O my God, in Thee I trust,
Let me not be put to shame;
Let not my enemies exult over me.
Yea, let none that wait for Thee be put to shame;
Let them be ashamed who are wantonly treacherous.

Make me to know Thy ways, O Lord;
Teach me Thy paths.
Lead me in Thy truth, and teach me,
For Thou art the God of my salvation;
For Thee I wait all the day long.

Be mindful of Thy mercy, O Lord, and of Thy steadfast love,
For they have been from of old.
Remember not the sins of my youth, or my transgressions;
According to Thy steadfast love remember me,
For Thy goodness' sake, O Lord!...

For thy name's sake, O Lord,
Pardon my guilt, for it is great.
Who is the man that fears the Lord?
Him will He instruct in the way that he should choose.
He himself shall abide in prosperity,
And his children shall possess the land.

Prayer Goals

Prayer Intentions

For whom or what do I want to pray this week? Anyone who frustrates me, or has caused harm to myself or those I love. Anyone/anything who has touched my heart.

"Not all of us can do great things. But we can do *small things with great love.*"
-Mother Teresa of Calcutta

My "small things" this week:

Checklist

We draw a box next to any goals we want to make for ourselves this week, and check them off as we go.

Morning Offering

Evening Prayer or Liturgy of the Hours

Daily/Weekly Rosary

Angelus

Scripture Reading

Divine Mercy Chaplet

Other: _____

Weekday/Daily Mass

Confession

Fasting

Read a Saint Biography

Give alms or a donation

Novena

Volunteer at Homeless Shelter or Food Bank
(or other Corporal Work of Mercy)

first, Breathe

Breathe in ...
7 seconds.
Hold your breath ...
7 seconds.
Breathe out ...
7 seconds.

Repeat.

As many times
as you like.

second, Become aware of God's Presence

third, Thanksgiving

Lord, I realize that all, even myself, is a gift from you. Today, for what things am I most grateful?

fourth,
Reflect

Psalm 4:8

"I will not mistrust Him, Meg, though I shall feel myself weakening and on the verge of being overcome with fear. I shall remember how Saint Peter, at a blast of wind, began to sink because of his lack of faith and I shall do as he did, call upon Christ and pray to Him for help. And then I trust He shall place His holy hand on me and... hold me up from drowning."
– St. Thomas More (to his daughter from prison)

fifth,
Examination

Lord, open my eyes and ears to be more honest with myself. Show me what has been happening to me and in me this day. Today, how have I experienced your love?

_____

_____

_____

_____

_____

_____

_____

_____

_____

_____

sixth
Contrition

Today, what choices have been inadequate responses to your love?

_____

_____

_____

_____

_____

seventh,
Hope

Lord, let me look with longing toward the future. How will I let you lead me to a brighter tomorrow?

_____

_____

_____

_____

_____

Weekly *Prayer*

Prayer for Our Families to Lead Lives Worthy of the Lord, Colossians 1:9-14

I pray that you may be filled with the knowledge of his will in all spiritual wisdom and understanding, to lead a life worthy of the Lord, fully pleasing to him, bearing fruit in every good work and increasing in the knowledge of God. May you be strengthened with all power, according to his glorious might, for all endurance and patience with joy, giving thanks to the Father, who has qualified us to share in the inheritance of the saints in light. He has delivered us from the dominion of darkness and transferred us to the kingdom of his beloved Son, in whom we have redemption, the forgiveness of sins. Amen.

Prayer Goals

Prayer Intentions

For whom or what do I want to pray this week? Anyone who frustrates me, or has caused harm to myself or those I love. Anyone/anything who has touched my heart.

_____
_____
_____
_____
_____
_____
_____
_____
_____
_____
_____

> "Not all of us can do great things. But we can do
> _small things with great love._"
> -Mother Teresa of Calcutta

My "small things" this week:

_____
_____
_____
_____
_____
_____
_____
_____
_____
_____
_____
_____
_____

Checklist

We draw a box next to any goals we want to make for ourselves this week, and check them off as we go.

Morning Offering

Evening Prayer or Liturgy of the Hours

Daily/Weekly Rosary

Angelus

Scripture Reading

Divine Mercy Chaplet

Other: _____

Weekday/Daily Mass

Confession

Fasting

Read a Saint Biography

Give alms or a donation

Novena

Volunteer at Homeless Shelter or Food Bank
(or other Corporal Work of Mercy)

first,
Breathe

Breathe in ...
7 seconds.
Hold your breath ...
7 seconds.
Breathe out ...
7 seconds.

Repeat.

As many times
as you like.

second,
Become aware of
God's Presence

third,
Thanksgiving

Lord, I realize that all, even myself, is a gift from you. Today, for what things am I most grateful?

fourth,
Reflect

Luke 10:41-42

"Unshakable peace does not come from getting through a certain amount of (work) over a specified amount of time, but it also doesn't come from throwing in the towel and giving in when things get hard. Peace comes from recognizing that our real task is to wake up each day and get our marching orders from God. It comes from diligence to the work He hands us. It comes from diligence infused with faith...
–Sarah Mackenzie

fifth,
Examination

Lord, open my eyes and ears to be more honest with myself. Show me what has been happening to me and in me this day. Today, how have I experienced your love?

_____
_____
_____
_____
_____
_____
_____
_____
_____
_____
_____
_____

sixth,
Contrition

Today, what choices have been inadequate responses to your love?

seventh,
Hope

Lord, let me look with longing toward the future. How will I let you lead me to a brighter tomorrow?

_____
_____
_____
_____
_____
_____

Weekly
Prayer

Prayer to Choose the Better Portion
by Mary Nadeau Reed

Lord Jesus,
You do not ask a thousand things of me.
You ask me to do one thing:
My calling in this moment, whatever it may be.
Give me wisdom to see what that is.
Free my mind of the need to accomplish and check off tasks.
Whisper to my heart what it is you want of me now.
Help me to sit at your feet
By being present to my family,
By speaking truth and wisdom to my children,
By living that truth and wisdom in how I care for their needs.
Release me from a frantic or overwhelmed mind.
Help me to see you in the now,
In the way you call me to sit at your feet at this moment.
Whether it's talking to my children, preparing a meal, paying bills.
Help me to find the good portion, the portion Mary chose,
and do not let me take it from myself.
Amen.

Prayer Goals

Prayer Intentions

For whom or what do I want to pray this week? Anyone who frustrates me, or has caused harm to myself or those I love. Anyone/anything who has touched my heart.

_____
_____
_____
_____
_____
_____
_____
_____
_____

"Not all of us can do great things. But we can do *small things with great love.*"
-Mother Teresa of Calcutta

My "small things" this week:

_____
_____
_____
_____
_____
_____
_____
_____
_____
_____
_____
_____
_____
_____
_____

Checklist

We draw a box next to any goals we want to make for ourselves this week, and check them off as we go.

Morning Offering

Evening Prayer or Liturgy of the Hours

Daily/Weekly Rosary

Angelus

Scripture Reading

Divine Mercy Chaplet

Other: _____

Weekday/Daily Mass

Confession

Fasting

Read a Saint Biography

Give alms or a donation

Novena

Volunteer at Homeless Shelter or Food Bank
(or other Corporal Work of Mercy)

first, Breathe

Breathe in ...
7 seconds.
Hold your breath ...
7 seconds.
Breathe out ...
7 seconds.

Repeat.

As many times
as you like.

second, Become aware of God's Presence

third, Thanksgiving

Lord, I realize that all, even myself, is a gift from you. Today, for what things am I most grateful?

fourth, *Reflect*

Romans 12:9-10

"The true test of character is not how much we know how to do, but how we behave when we don't know what to do."
–John Holt

fifth, Examination

Lord, open my eyes and ears to be more honest with myself. Show me what has been happening to me and in me this day. Today, how have I experienced your love?

_____

_____

_____

_____

_____

_____

_____

_____

_____

_____

_____

_____

_____

_____

sixth Contrition

Today, what choices have been inadequate responses to your love?

_____

_____

_____

_____

_____

_____

_____

seventh, Hope

Lord, let me look with longing toward the future. How will I let you lead me to a brighter tomorrow?

_____

_____

_____

_____

_____

_____

_____

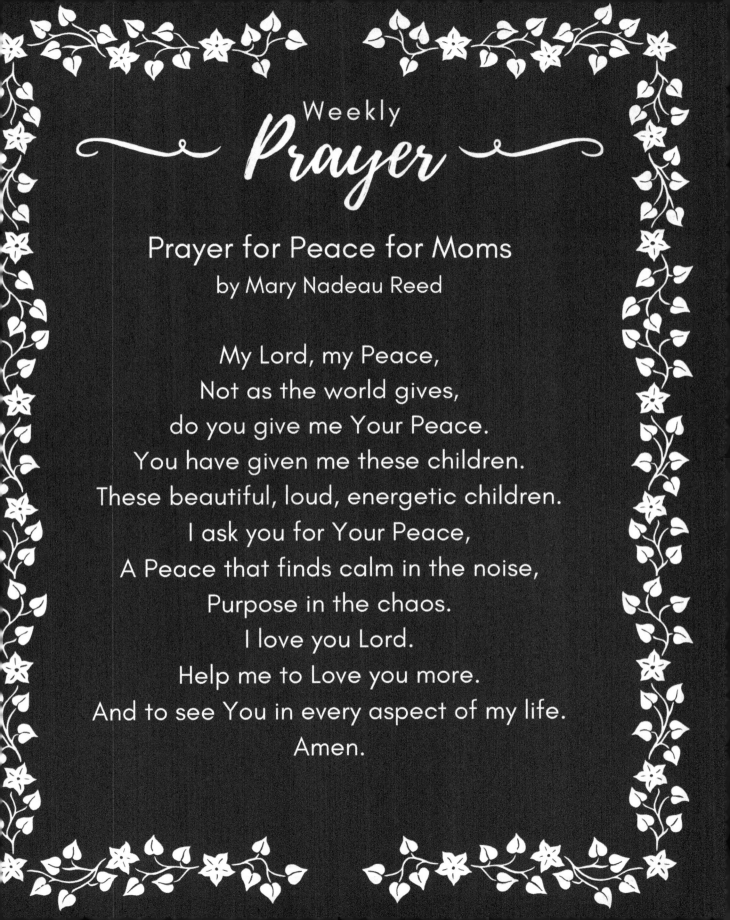

Weekly *Prayer*

Prayer for Peace for Moms
by Mary Nadeau Reed

My Lord, my Peace,
Not as the world gives,
do you give me Your Peace.
You have given me these children.
These beautiful, loud, energetic children.
I ask you for Your Peace,
A Peace that finds calm in the noise,
Purpose in the chaos.
I love you Lord.
Help me to Love you more.
And to see You in every aspect of my life.
Amen.

Prayer Goals

Prayer Intentions

For whom or what do I want to pray this week? Anyone who frustrates me, or has caused harm to myself or those I love. Anyone/anything who has touched my heart.

_____
_____
_____
_____
_____
_____
_____

"Not all of us can do great things. But we can do *small things with great love.*"
-Mother Teresa of Calcutta

My "small things" this week:

_____
_____
_____
_____
_____
_____
_____
_____
_____
_____

Checklist

We draw a box next to any goals we want to make for ourselves this week, and check them off as we go.

Morning Offering

Evening Prayer or Liturgy of the Hours

Daily/Weekly Rosary

Angelus

Scripture Reading

Divine Mercy Chaplet

Other: _____

Weekday/Daily Mass

Confession

Fasting

Read a Saint Biography

Give alms or a donation

Novena

Volunteer at Homeless Shelter or Food Bank
(or other Corporal Work of Mercy)

first, Breathe

Breathe in ...
7 seconds.
Hold your breath ...
7 seconds.
Breathe out ...
7 seconds.

Repeat.

As many times
as you like.

second, Become aware of God's Presence

third, Thanksgiving

Lord, I realize that all, even myself, is a gift from you. Today, for what things am I most grateful?

fourth, Reflect

Matthew 6:25-27

"The great thing, if one can, is to stop regarding all the unpleasant things as interruptions of one's 'own', or 'real' life. The truth is of course that what one calls the interruptions are precisely one's real life – the life God is sending one day by day; what one calls one's 'real life' is a phantom of one's own imagination." – C.S. Lewis, *Letters of C.S. Lewis*

fifth, Examination

Lord, open my eyes and ears to be more honest with myself. Show me what has been happening to me and in me this day. Today, how have I experienced your love?

_____
_____
_____
_____
_____
_____
_____
_____
_____
_____
_____
_____
_____

sixth Contrition

Today, what choices have been inadequate responses to your love?

_____
_____
_____
_____
_____
_____
_____

seventh, Hope

Lord, let me look with longing toward the future. How will I let you lead me to a brighter tomorrow?

_____
_____
_____
_____
_____
_____
_____

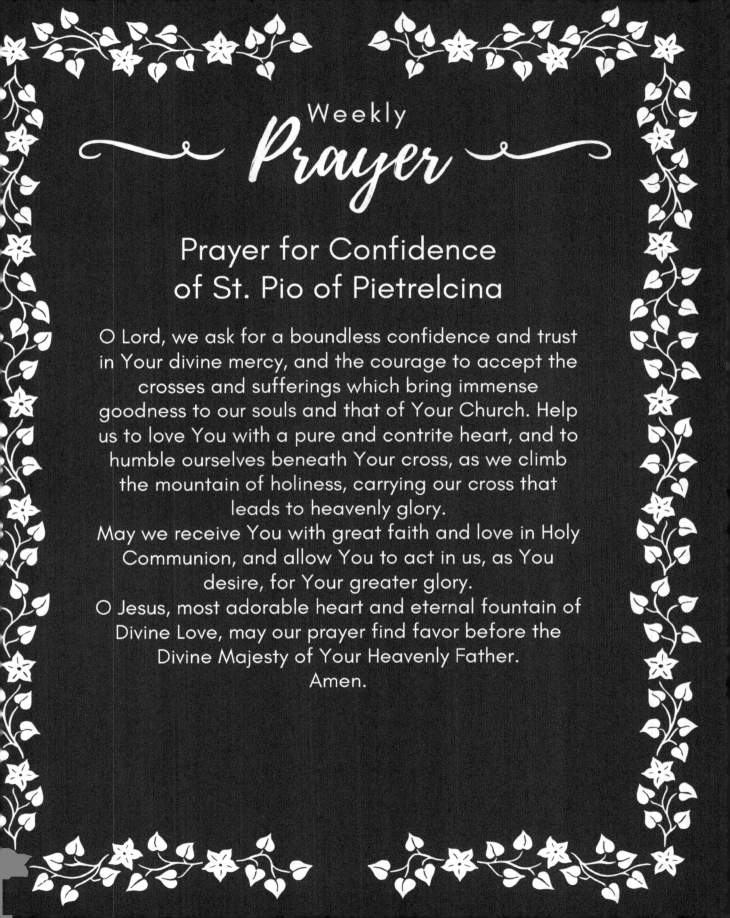

Weekly *Prayer*

Prayer for Confidence of St. Pio of Pietrelcina

O Lord, we ask for a boundless confidence and trust in Your divine mercy, and the courage to accept the crosses and sufferings which bring immense goodness to our souls and that of Your Church. Help us to love You with a pure and contrite heart, and to humble ourselves beneath Your cross, as we climb the mountain of holiness, carrying our cross that leads to heavenly glory.

May we receive You with great faith and love in Holy Communion, and allow You to act in us, as You desire, for Your greater glory.

O Jesus, most adorable heart and eternal fountain of Divine Love, may our prayer find favor before the Divine Majesty of Your Heavenly Father.
Amen.

Prayer Goals

Prayer Intentions

For whom or what do I want to pray this week? Anyone who frustrates me, or has caused harm to myself or those I love. Anyone/anything who has touched my heart.

_____
_____
_____
_____
_____

"Not all of us can do great things. But we can do _small things with great love._"
-Mother Teresa of Calcutta

My "small things" this week:

_____
_____
_____

Checklist

We draw a box next to any goals we want to make for ourselves this week, and check them off as we go.

_____
_____
_____
_____
_____
_____
_____
_____
_____

Morning Offering

Evening Prayer or Liturgy of the Hours

Daily/Weekly Rosary

Angelus

Scripture Reading

Divine Mercy Chaplet

Other: _____

Weekday/Daily Mass

Confession

Fasting

Read a Saint Biography

Give alms or a donation

Novena

Volunteer at Homeless Shelter or Food Bank
(or other Corporal Work of Mercy)

first, Breathe

Breathe in ...
7 seconds.
Hold your breath ...
7 seconds.
Breathe out ...
7 seconds.

Repeat.

As many times
as you like.

second, Become aware of God's Presence

third, Thanksgiving

Lord, I realize that all, even myself, is a gift from you. Today, for what things am I most grateful?

fourth,
Reflect

Philippians 4:8

"During times of universal deceit, telling the truth becomes a revolutionary act."
-George Orwell

fifth,
Examination

Lord, open my eyes and ears to be more honest with myself. Show me what has been happening to me and in me this day. Today, how have I experienced your love?

_____

_____

_____

_____

_____

_____

_____

_____

sixth
Contrition

Today, what choices have been inadequate responses to your love?

_____

_____

_____

_____

_____

seventh,
Hope

Lord, let me look with longing toward the future. How will I let you lead me to a brighter tomorrow?

_____

_____

_____

_____

_____

Weekly
Prayer

Prayer to Always Teach My Children the Truth
by Mary Nadeau Reed

My Jesus,
Our children are growing up in a world of many voices.
Many call evil "good", and good "evil."
I want to give my children a better world
By living in Your Truth,
I dare to hope that they will make this world a better place,
And even more so, I hope for them to attain life eternal in the
world beyond this one;
In the world their hearts were made for.

Lord, You are the Way, the Truth, the Life,
Give me boldness and wisdom to communicate your Truth
In a way that it will be received with joy by Your little ones.
Let Your Ways take root in their hearts.
Let Your Light shine forth from their lives.

We praise you for the honor of teaching our children the Truth.
We thank you for the blessing of living in a time and place
Where we can do so without putting our physical safety at risk.
However, even if that should change,
Whatever the future may bring, be it good or ill,
Please strengthen us and guide us in speaking Your Words,
And open the ears of our children to receive You into their hearts.
Amen.

Prayer Goals

Prayer Intentions

For whom or what do I want to pray this week? Anyone who frustrates me, or has caused harm to myself or those I love. Anyone/anything who has touched my heart.

"Not all of us can do great things. But we can do *small things with great love.*"

-Mother Teresa of Calcutta

My "small things" this week:

Checklist

We draw a box next to any goals we want to make for ourselves this week, and check them off as we go.

Morning Offering

Evening Prayer or Liturgy of the Hours

Daily/Weekly Rosary

Angelus

Scripture Reading

Divine Mercy Chaplet

Other: _____

Weekday/Daily Mass

Confession

Fasting

Read a Saint Biography

Give alms or a donation

Novena

Volunteer at Homeless Shelter or Food Bank
(or other Corporal Work of Mercy)

first, Breathe

Breathe in ...
7 seconds.
Hold your breath ...
7 seconds.
Breathe out ...
7 seconds.

Repeat.

As many times
as you like.

second, Become aware of God's Presence

third, Thanksgiving

Lord, I realize that all, even myself, is a gift from you. Today, for what things am I most grateful?

fourth, Reflect

Jeremiah 29:11

"Never be afraid to trust an unknown future to a known God."
–Corrie Ten Boom (Concentration Camp Survivor, Christian Writer/Speaker)

fifth, Examination

Lord, open my eyes and ears to be more honest with myself. Show me what has been happening to me and in me this day. Today, how have I experienced your love?

_____
_____
_____
_____
_____
_____
_____
_____
_____
_____
_____
_____
_____
_____

sixth, Contrition

Today, what choices have been inadequate responses to your love?

_____
_____
_____
_____
_____
_____
_____

seventh, Hope

Lord, let me look with longing toward the future. How will I let you lead me to a brighter tomorrow?

_____
_____
_____
_____
_____
_____
_____

Weekly
Prayer

Prayer for Trust
of St. Ignatius of Loyola

O Christ Jesus
When all is darkness
And we feel our weakness and
helplessness,
Give us the sense of Your Presence,
Your Love and Your Strength.
Help us to have perfect trust
In Your protecting love
And strengthening power,
So that nothing may frighten or worry us,
For, living close to You,
We shall see Your Hand,
Your Purpose, Your Will through all things.

Prayer Goals

Prayer Intentions

For whom or what do I want to pray this week? Anyone who frustrates me, or has caused harm to myself or those I love. Anyone/anything who has touched my heart.

"Not all of us can do great things. But we can do *small things with great love.*"
—Mother Teresa of Calcutta

My "small things" this week:

Checklist

We draw a box next to any goals we want to make for ourselves this week, and check them off as we go.

- Morning Offering
- Evening Prayer or Liturgy of the Hours
- Daily/Weekly Rosary
- Angelus
- Scripture Reading
- Divine Mercy Chaplet
- Other: _____

- Weekday/Daily Mass
- Confession
- Fasting
- Read a Saint Biography
- Give alms or a donation
- Novena
- Volunteer at Homeless Shelter or Food Bank
(or other Corporal Work of Mercy)

first, Breathe

Breathe in ...
7 seconds.
Hold your breath ...
7 seconds.
Breathe out ...
7 seconds.

Repeat.

As many times
as you like.

second, Become aware of God's Presence

third, Thanksgiving

Lord, I realize that all, even myself, is a gift from you. Today, for what things am I most grateful?

fourth,
Reflect

John 14:27

"Peace is experienced by the one who allows himself to be loved."
– Chiara Corbella Petrillo, Servant of God

fifth,
Examination

Lord, open my eyes and ears to be more honest with myself. Show me what has been happening to me and in me this day. Today, how have I experienced your love?

_____
_____
_____
_____
_____
_____
_____
_____
_____
_____

sixth
Contrition

Today, what choices have been inadequate responses to your love?

_____
_____
_____
_____
_____
_____

seventh,
Hope

Lord, let me look with longing toward the future. How will I let you lead me to a brighter tomorrow?

_____
_____
_____
_____
_____
_____

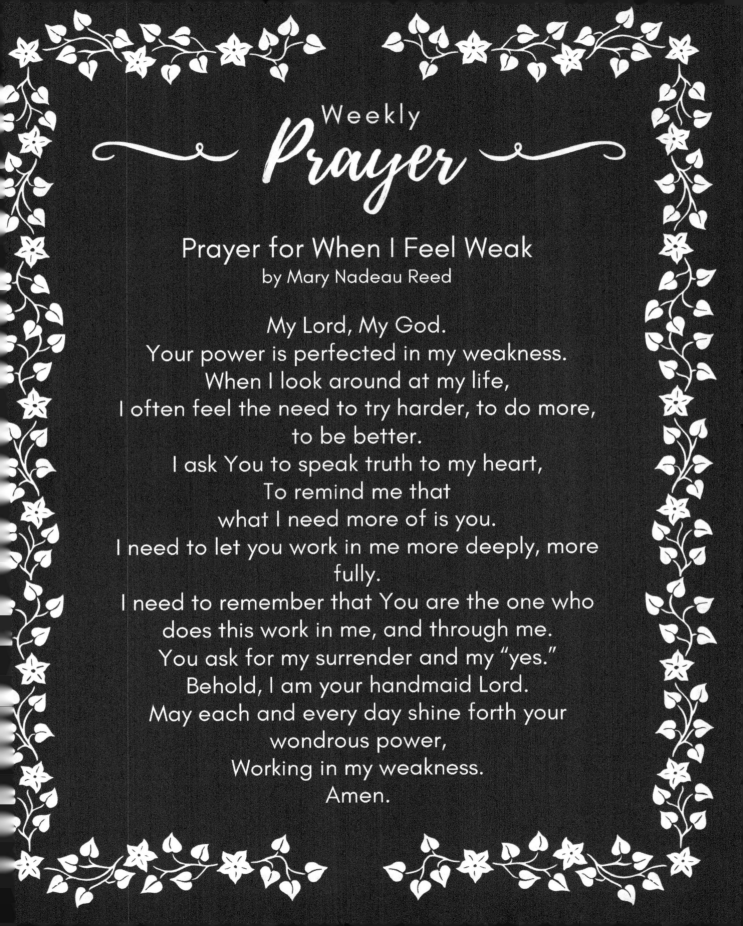

Weekly
Prayer

Prayer for When I Feel Weak
by Mary Nadeau Reed

My Lord, My God.
Your power is perfected in my weakness.
When I look around at my life,
I often feel the need to try harder, to do more,
to be better.
I ask You to speak truth to my heart,
To remind me that
what I need more of is you.
I need to let you work in me more deeply, more
fully.
I need to remember that You are the one who
does this work in me, and through me.
You ask for my surrender and my "yes."
Behold, I am your handmaid Lord.
May each and every day shine forth your
wondrous power,
Working in my weakness.
Amen.

Prayer Goals

Prayer Intentions

For whom or what do I want to pray this week? Anyone who frustrates me, or has caused harm to myself or those I love. Anyone/anything who has touched my heart.

_____
_____
_____
_____
_____
_____
_____

"Not all of us can do great things. But we can do *small things with great love.*"
-Mother Teresa of Calcutta

My "small things" this week:

_____
_____
_____
_____
_____
_____
_____
_____
_____
_____
_____
_____
_____

Checklist

We draw a box next to any goals we want to make for ourselves this week, and check them off as we go.

Morning Offering

Evening Prayer or Liturgy of the Hours

Daily/Weekly Rosary

Angelus

Scripture Reading

Divine Mercy Chaplet

Other: _____

Weekday/Daily Mass

Confession

Fasting

Read a Saint Biography

Give alms or a donation

Novena

Volunteer at Homeless Shelter or Food Bank
(or other Corporal Work of Mercy)

first, Breathe

Breathe in ...
7 seconds.
Hold your breath ...
7 seconds.
Breathe out ...
7 seconds.

Repeat.

As many times
as you like.

second, Become aware of God's Presence

third, Thanksgiving

Lord, I realize that all, even myself, is a gift from you. Today, for what things am I most grateful?

fourth,
Reflect

1 Corinthians 16:14

"If you want to change the world, first go home and love your family."
–St. Teresa of Calcutta

fifth,
Examination

Lord, open my eyes and ears to be more honest with myself. Show me what has been happening to me and in me this day. Today, how have I experienced your love?

_____
_____
_____
_____
_____
_____
_____
_____
_____
_____
_____
_____
_____
_____
_____

sixth,
Contrition

Today, what choices have been inadequate responses to your love?

_____
_____
_____
_____
_____
_____
_____
_____

seventh,
Hope

Lord, let me look with longing toward the future. How will I let you lead me to a brighter tomorrow?

_____
_____
_____
_____
_____
_____
_____
_____

Weekly Prayer

Prayer of St. Teresa of Calcutta for the Family

Heavenly Father,
you have given us a model of life in the Holy Family of Nazareth.
Help us, O Loving Father, to make our family another Nazareth
where love, peace and joy reign.
May it be deeply contemplative, intensely Eucharistic and vibrant with joy.
Help us to stay together in joy and sorrow through family prayer.
Teach us to see Jesus in the members of our family,
especially in their distressing disguise.
May the Eucharistic Heart of Jesus
make our hearts meek and humble like His,
and help us to carry out our family duties in a holy way.
May we love one another as God loves each one of us,
more and more each day,
and forgive each other's faults as you forgive our sins.
Help us, O Loving Father,
to take whatever you give, and to give whatever you take, with a big
smile. Help us, O Holy Father, to make our families one heart, full of love,
in the Heart of Jesus through Mary.
Immaculate Heart of Mary, cause of our joy, pray for us.
St. Joseph, pray for us.
Holy Guardian Angels, be always with us, guide and protect us.
Amen.

Prayer Goals

Prayer Intentions

For whom or what do I want to pray this week? Anyone who frustrates me, or has caused harm to myself or those I love. Anyone/anything who has touched my heart.

_____

_____

_____

_____

_____

_____

"Not all of us can do great things. But we can do

small things with great love."
-Mother Teresa of Calcutta

My "small things" this week:

_____

_____

_____

_____

_____

Checklist

We draw a box next to any goals we want to make for ourselves this week, and check them off as we go.

Morning Offering

Evening Prayer or Liturgy of the Hours

Daily/Weekly Rosary

Angelus

Scripture Reading

Divine Mercy Chaplet

Other: _____

Weekday/Daily Mass

Confession

Fasting

Read a Saint Biography

Give alms or a donation

Novena

Volunteer at Homeless Shelter or Food Bank
(or other Corporal Work of Mercy)

_____

_____

_____

_____

_____

_____

_____

_____

first, Breathe

Breathe in ...
7 seconds.
Hold your breath ...
7 seconds.
Breathe out ...
7 seconds.

Repeat.

As many times
as you like.

second, Become aware of God's Presence

third, Thanksgiving

Lord, I realize that all, even myself, is a gift from you. Today, for what things am I most grateful?

fourth,
Reflect

1 Peter 5:7

"Success is not final, failure is not fatal:
it is the courage to continue that counts."
–Winston S. Churchill

fifth,
Examination

Lord, open my eyes and ears to be more honest with myself. Show me what has been happening to me and in me this day. Today, how have I experienced your love?

_____
_____
_____
_____
_____
_____
_____
_____
_____
_____
_____

sixth
Contrition

Today, what choices have been inadequate responses to your love?

_____
_____
_____
_____
_____
_____

seventh,
Hope

Lord, let me look with longing toward the future. How will I let you lead me to a brighter tomorrow?

_____
_____
_____
_____
_____
_____

Prayer

Traditional Act of Hope

My God, relying on your
infinite goodness and promises,
I hope to obtain pardon of my sins,
Help of your grace,
And life everlasting
Through the merits of Jesus Christ,
My Lord and Redeemer
Amen.

Prayer Goals

Prayer Intentions

For whom or what do I want to pray this week? Anyone who frustrates me, or has caused harm to myself or those I love. Anyone/anything who has touched my heart.

_____
_____
_____
_____
_____
_____
_____
_____
_____

"Not all of us can do great things. But we can do

small things with great love."

-Mother Teresa of Calcutta

My "small things" this week:

_____
_____
_____
_____
_____

Checklist

We draw a box next to any goals we want to make for ourselves this week, and check them off as we go.

_____
_____
_____
_____
_____
_____
_____
_____

Morning Offering

Evening Prayer or Liturgy of the Hours

Daily/Weekly Rosary

Angelus

Scripture Reading

Divine Mercy Chaplet

Other: _____

Weekday/Daily Mass

Confession

Fasting

Read a Saint Biography

Give alms or a donation

Novena

Volunteer at Homeless Shelter or Food Bank
(or other Corporal Work of Mercy)

Week Eighteen

first, Breathe

Breathe in ...
7 seconds.
Hold your breath ...
7 seconds.
Breathe out ...
7 seconds.

Repeat.

As many times
as you like.

second,
Become aware of
God's Presence

third,
Thanksgiving

Lord, I realize that all, even myself, is a gift from you. Today, for what things am I most grateful?

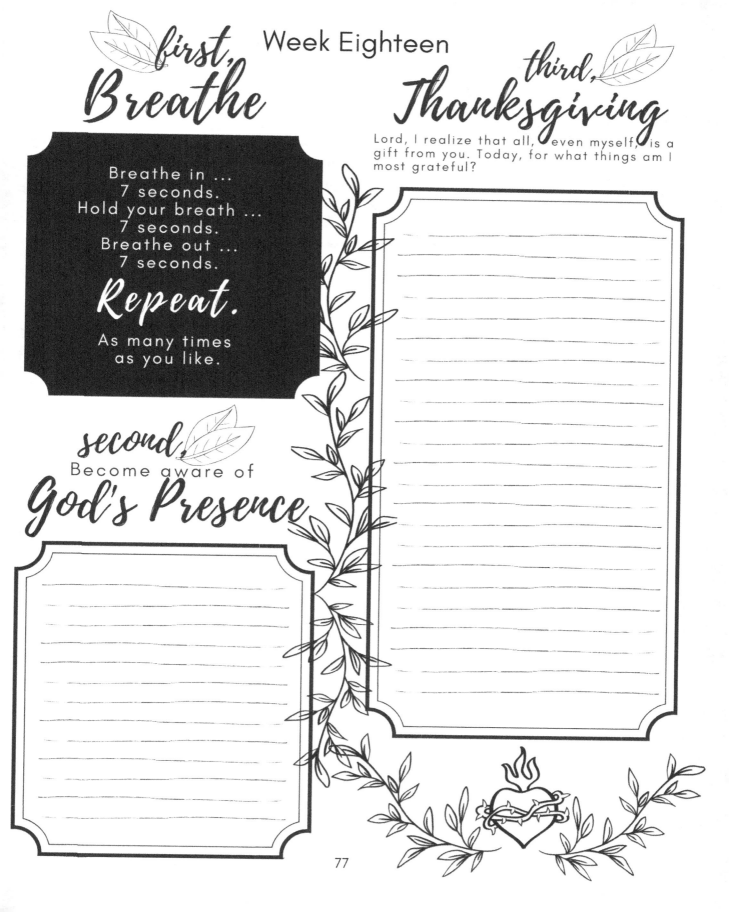

fourth, Reflect

1 Corinthians 13:4-7

"If a man does not keep pace with his companions, perhaps it is because he hears a different drummer. Let him step to the music which he hears, however measured or far away." – Henry David Thoreau

fifth, Examination

Lord, open my eyes and ears to be more honest with myself. Show me what has been happening to me and in me this day. Today, how have I experienced your love?

_____
_____
_____
_____
_____
_____
_____
_____
_____
_____
_____

sixth, Contrition

Today, what choices have been inadequate responses to your love?

_____
_____
_____
_____
_____
_____

seventh, Hope

Lord, let me look with longing toward the future. How will I let you lead me to a brighter tomorrow?

_____
_____
_____
_____
_____
_____

Weekly
Prayer

Prayer to Go at the Lord's Pace
by Mary Nadeau Reed

Dear Lord,
I have my plans, my desires.
I want to get through life at the pace
that seems reasonable to me.
But you haven't given me computers or robots to raise.
You've given me human children.
They do not follow a pattern
or develop at an equal pace.
Just as I don't learn the lessons
that you try to teach me the first time,
And I am still learning to see you
and your will in my life.
Help me to see them with your eyes.
Eyes of patience, of presence.
Help me to challenge them, to avoid complacency,
While showing me the way to nurture their hearts,
their curiosity,
Their faith, and their relationships with others.
Let me love them as they are,
But too much to leave them there,
Patiently enough to grow at your pace, and theirs.
Amen.

Prayer Goals

Prayer Intentions

For whom or what do I want to pray this week? Anyone who frustrates me, or has caused harm to myself or those I love. Anyone/anything who has touched my heart.

_____
_____
_____
_____
_____
_____

"Not all of us can do great things. But we can do *small things with great love.*"
—Mother Teresa of Calcutta

My "small things" this week:

_____
_____

Checklist

We draw a box next to any goals we want to make for ourselves this week, and check them off as we go.

Morning Offering

Evening Prayer or Liturgy of the Hours

Daily/Weekly Rosary

Angelus

Scripture Reading

Divine Mercy Chaplet

Other: _____

Weekday/Daily Mass

Confession

Fasting

Read a Saint Biography

Give alms or a donation

Novena

Volunteer at Homeless Shelter or Food Bank
(or other Corporal Work of Mercy)

_____
_____
_____
_____
_____
_____
_____
_____
_____

first, Breathe

Breathe in ...
7 seconds.
Hold your breath ...
7 seconds.
Breathe out ...
7 seconds.

Repeat.

As many times
as you like.

second, Become aware of God's Presence

third, Thanksgiving

Lord, I realize that all, even myself, is a gift from you. Today, for what things am I most grateful?

fourth,
Reflect

1 Corinthians 13:13

"She is no fool who gives what she cannot keep to gain what she cannot lose." – St. Edith Stein

fifth,
Examination

Lord, open my eyes and ears to be more honest with myself. Show me what has been happening to me and in me this day. Today, how have I experienced your love?

_____
_____
_____
_____
_____
_____
_____
_____
_____
_____
_____
_____

sixth
Contrition

Today, what choices have been inadequate responses to your love?

_____
_____
_____
_____
_____
_____

seventh,
Hope

Lord, let me look with longing toward the future. How will I let you lead me to a brighter tomorrow?

_____
_____
_____
_____
_____
_____

Weekly
Prayer

Surrender Prayer
of St. Ignatius of Loyola

Take, Lord, and receive all my liberty,
My memory, my understanding,
And my entire will –
All that I have and call my own.
You have given it all to me.
To you, Lord, I return it.
Everything is yours;
Do with it what you will.
Give me only your love and your grace.
That is enough for me.
Amen.

Prayer Goals

Prayer Intentions

For whom or what do I want to pray this week? Anyone who frustrates me, or has caused harm to myself or those I love. Anyone/anything who has touched my heart.

_____
_____
_____
_____
_____
_____
_____
_____
_____

"Not all of us can do great things. But we can do *small things with great love.*"

-Mother Teresa of Calcutta

My "small things" this week:

_____
_____
_____
_____
_____
_____
_____
_____
_____
_____
_____
_____
_____

Checklist

We draw a box next to any goals we want to make for ourselves this week, and check them off as we go.

Morning Offering

Evening Prayer or Liturgy of the Hours

Daily/Weekly Rosary

Angelus

Scripture Reading

Divine Mercy Chaplet

Other: _____

Weekday/Daily Mass

Confession

Fasting

Read a Saint Biography

Give alms or a donation

Novena

Volunteer at Homeless Shelter or Food Bank
(or other Corporal Work of Mercy)

first, Breathe

Breathe in ...
7 seconds.
Hold your breath ...
7 seconds.
Breathe out ...
7 seconds.

Repeat.

As many times
as you like.

second,
Become aware of
God's Presence

third, Thanksgiving

Lord, I realize that all, even myself, is a gift from you. Today, for what things am I most grateful?

fourth, Reflect

Colossians 3:2-4

"God can't give us peace and happiness apart from Himself because there is no such thing." - C.S. Lewis

fifth, Examination

Lord, open my eyes and ears to be more honest with myself. Show me what has been happening to me and in me this day. Today, how have I experienced your love?

_____

_____

_____

_____

_____

_____

_____

_____

_____

_____

_____

_____

_____

_____

_____

_____

sixth, Contrition

Today, what choices have been inadequate responses to your love?

_____

_____

_____

_____

_____

_____

seventh, Hope

Lord, let me look with longing toward the future. How will I let you lead me to a brighter tomorrow?

_____

_____

_____

_____

_____

_____

Weekly *Prayer*

Prayer of St. Francis of Assisi

Lord, make me an instrument of your peace:
where there is hatred, let me sow love;
where there is injury, pardon;
where there is doubt, faith;
where there is despair, hope;
where there is darkness, light;
where there is sadness, joy.

O Divine Master, grant that I may not so much seek
to be consoled as to console,
to be understood as to understand,
to be loved as to love.
For it is in giving that we receive,
it is in pardoning that we are pardoned,
and it is in dying that we are born to eternal life.
Amen.

Prayer Goals

Prayer Intentions

For whom or what do I want to pray this week? Anyone who frustrates me, or has caused harm to myself or those I love. Anyone/anything who has touched my heart.

_____
_____
_____
_____
_____
_____
_____
_____

"Not all of us can do great things. But we can do

small things with great love."

-Mother Teresa of Calcutta

My "small things" this week:

_____
_____
_____
_____
_____
_____
_____
_____
_____
_____
_____

Checklist

We draw a box next to any goals we want to make for ourselves this week, and check them off as we go.

Morning Offering

Evening Prayer or Liturgy of the Hours

Daily/Weekly Rosary

Angelus

Scripture Reading

Divine Mercy Chaplet

Other: _____

Weekday/Daily Mass

Confession

Fasting

Read a Saint Biography

Give alms or a donation

Novena

Volunteer at Homeless Shelter or Food Bank
(or other Corporal Work of Mercy)

first, Breathe

Breathe in ...
7 seconds.
Hold your breath ...
7 seconds.
Breathe out ...
7 seconds.

Repeat.

As many times
as you like.

second, Become aware of *God's Presence*

third, Thanksgiving

Lord, I realize that all, even myself, is a gift from you. Today, for what things am I most grateful?

fourth,
Reflect

Ephesians 3:16-17

"Let no one mourn that he has fallen again and again,
for Forgiveness has risen from the grave!"
– St. John Chrysostom

fifth,
Examination

Lord, open my eyes and ears to be more honest with myself. Show me what has been happening to me and in me this day. Today, how have I experienced your love?

_____
_____
_____
_____
_____
_____
_____
_____
_____
_____

sixth
Contrition

Today, what choices have been inadequate responses to your love?

seventh,
Hope

Lord, let me look with longing toward the future. How will I let you lead me to a brighter tomorrow?

_____
_____
_____
_____
_____

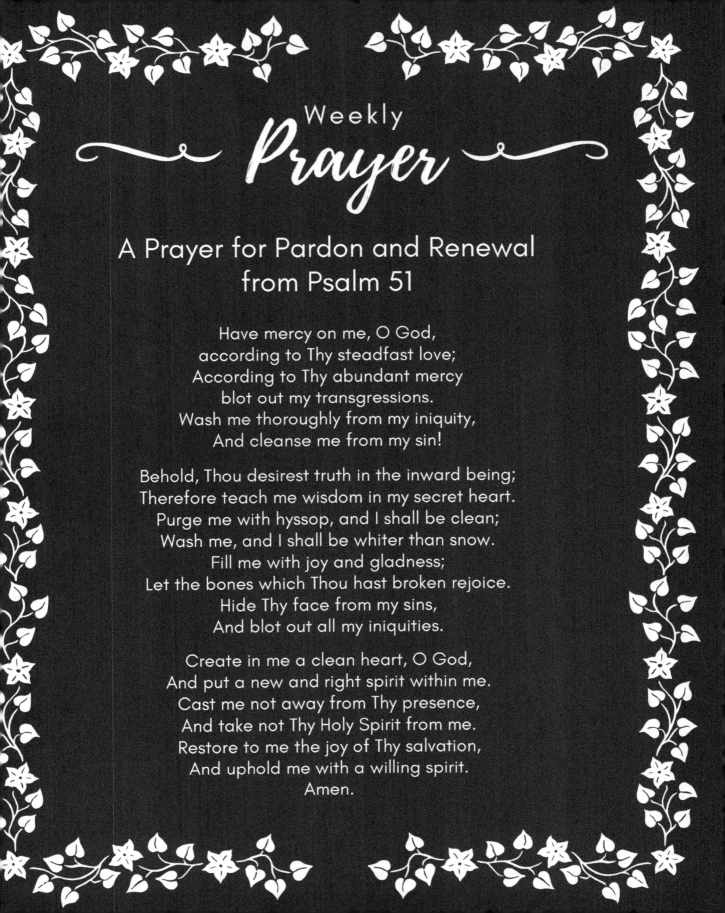

Weekly
Prayer

A Prayer for Pardon and Renewal
from Psalm 51

Have mercy on me, O God,
according to Thy steadfast love;
According to Thy abundant mercy
blot out my transgressions.
Wash me thoroughly from my iniquity,
And cleanse me from my sin!

Behold, Thou desirest truth in the inward being;
Therefore teach me wisdom in my secret heart.
Purge me with hyssop, and I shall be clean;
Wash me, and I shall be whiter than snow.
Fill me with joy and gladness;
Let the bones which Thou hast broken rejoice.
Hide Thy face from my sins,
And blot out all my iniquities.

Create in me a clean heart, O God,
And put a new and right spirit within me.
Cast me not away from Thy presence,
And take not Thy Holy Spirit from me.
Restore to me the joy of Thy salvation,
And uphold me with a willing spirit.
Amen.

Prayer Goals

Prayer Intentions

For whom or what do I want to pray this week? Anyone who frustrates me, or has caused harm to myself or those I love. Anyone/anything who has touched my heart.

"Not all of us can do great things. But we can do *small things with great love.*"
-Mother Teresa of Calcutta

My "small things" this week:

Checklist

We draw a box next to any goals we want to make for ourselves this week, and check them off as we go.

Morning Offering

Evening Prayer or Liturgy of the Hours

Daily/Weekly Rosary

Angelus

Scripture Reading

Divine Mercy Chaplet

Other: _____

Weekday/Daily Mass

Confession

Fasting

Read a Saint Biography

Give alms or a donation

Novena

Volunteer at Homeless Shelter or Food Bank
(or other Corporal Work of Mercy)

first, Breathe

Breathe in ...
7 seconds.
Hold your breath ...
7 seconds.
Breathe out ...
7 seconds.

Repeat.

As many times
as you like.

second, Become aware of God's Presence

third, Thanksgiving

Lord, I realize that all, even myself, is a gift from you. Today, for what things am I most grateful?

fourth, Reflect

John 15:13

"We should take as a maxim never to be surprised at current difficulties, no more than at a passing breeze, because with a little patience we shall see them disappear. Time changes everything." – St. Vincent de Paul

fifth, Examination

Lord, open my eyes and ears to be more honest with myself. Show me what has been happening to me and in me this day. Today, how have I experienced your love?

sixth, Contrition

Today, what choices have been inadequate responses to your love?

seventh, Hope

Lord, let me look with longing toward the future. How will I let you lead me to a brighter tomorrow?

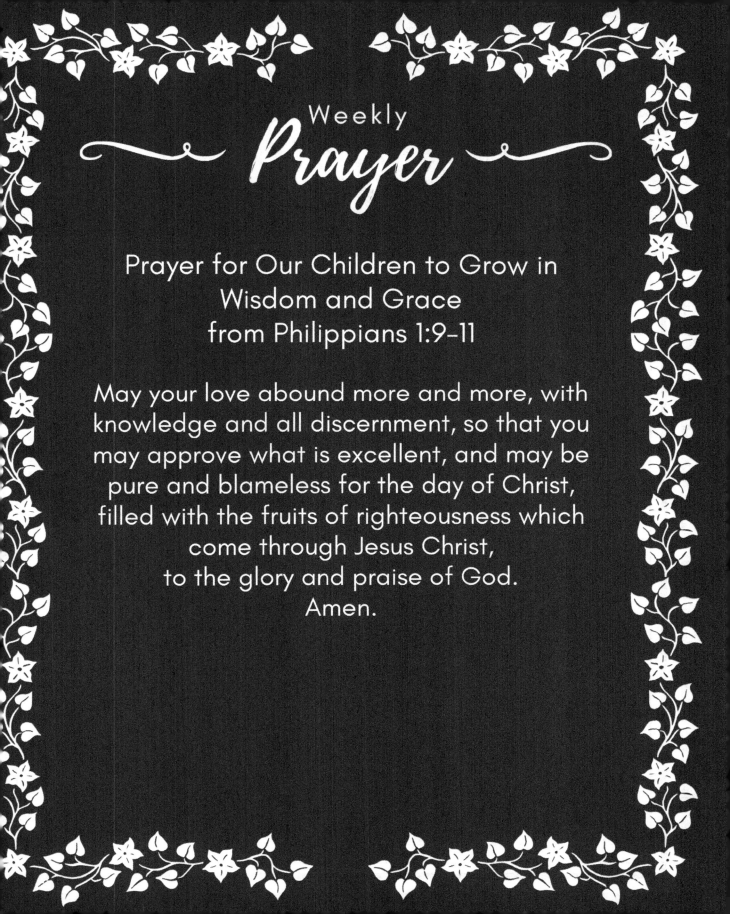

Weekly
Prayer

Prayer for Our Children to Grow in
Wisdom and Grace
from Philippians 1:9-11

May your love abound more and more, with
knowledge and all discernment, so that you
may approve what is excellent, and may be
pure and blameless for the day of Christ,
filled with the fruits of righteousness which
come through Jesus Christ,
to the glory and praise of God.
Amen.

Prayer Goals

Prayer Intentions

For whom or what do I want to pray this week? Anyone who frustrates me, or has caused harm to myself or those I love. Anyone/anything who has touched my heart.

_____
_____
_____
_____
_____
_____

"Not all of us can do great things. But we can do *small things with great love.*"
-Mother Teresa of Calcutta

My "small things" this week:

_____
_____
_____

Checklist

We draw a box next to any goals we want to make for ourselves this week, and check them off as we go.

_____
_____
_____
_____
_____
_____
_____
_____

Morning Offering

Evening Prayer or Liturgy of the Hours

Daily/Weekly Rosary

Angelus

Scripture Reading

Divine Mercy Chaplet

Other: _____

Weekday/Daily Mass

Confession

Fasting

Read a Saint Biography

Give alms or a donation

Novena

Volunteer at Homeless Shelter or Food Bank
(or other Corporal Work of Mercy)

first,
Breathe

Week Twenty-Three

third,
Thanksgiving

Lord, I realize that all, even myself, is a gift from you. Today, for what things am I most grateful?

Breathe in ...
7 seconds.
Hold your breath ...
7 seconds.
Breathe out ...
7 seconds.

Repeat.

As many times
as you like.

second,
Become aware of
God's Presence

fourth, Reflect

Isaiah 40:31

"Anticipate Beauty. Believe in miracles. Count on grace. Decide on joy. Expect peace." - Mary Davis

fifth, Examination

Lord, open my eyes and ears to be more honest with myself. Show me what has been happening to me and in me this day. Today, how have I experienced your love?

_____
_____
_____
_____
_____
_____
_____
_____
_____
_____
_____
_____

sixth, Contrition

Today, what choices have been inadequate responses to your love?

_____
_____
_____
_____
_____
_____

seventh, Hope

Lord, let me look with longing toward the future. How will I let you lead me to a brighter tomorrow?

_____
_____
_____
_____
_____
_____

Weekly
Prayer

Prayer for Joy
by Mary Nadeau Reed

Dear Lord Jesus,
You are Good.
We are Yours.
You are with us every day,
And you are preparing us to be happy
forever with You.
I ask you to give us
the Joy that only you can,
That we might always have
our eyes on You.
Amen.

Prayer Goals

Prayer Intentions

For whom or what do I want to pray this week? Anyone who frustrates me, or has caused harm to myself or those I love. Anyone/anything who has touched my heart.

_____
_____
_____
_____
_____
_____

> "Not all of us can do great things. But we can do
> *small things with great love.*"
> -Mother Teresa of Calcutta

My "small things" this week:

_____
_____

Checklist

We draw a box next to any goals we want to make for ourselves this week, and check them off as we go.

_____
_____
_____
_____
_____
_____
_____
_____
_____
_____
_____

Morning Offering

Evening Prayer or Liturgy of the Hours

Daily/Weekly Rosary

Angelus

Scripture Reading

Divine Mercy Chaplet

Other: _____

Weekday/Daily Mass

Confession

Fasting

Read a Saint Biography

Give alms or a donation

Novena

Volunteer at Homeless Shelter or Food Bank
(or other Corporal Work of Mercy)

first,
Breathe

Week Twenty-Four

third,
Thanksgiving

Lord, I realize that all, even myself, is a gift from you. Today, for what things am I most grateful?

Breathe in ...
7 seconds.
Hold your breath ...
7 seconds.
Breathe out ...
7 seconds.

Repeat.

As many times
as you like.

second,
Become aware of
God's Presence

fourth, Reflect

Matthew 10:28-31

"(Motherhood is the) ultimate career. All other careers exist for one purpose only – and that is to support the ultimate career."
-often attributed to C.S. Lewis

fifth, Examination

Lord, open my eyes and ears to be more honest with myself. Show me what has been happening to me and in me this day. Today, how have I experienced your love?

_____
_____
_____
_____
_____
_____
_____
_____
_____

sixth Contrition

Today, what choices have been inadequate responses to your love?

_____
_____
_____
_____
_____

seventh, Hope

Lord, let me look with longing toward the future. How will I let you lead me to a brighter tomorrow?

_____
_____
_____
_____
_____

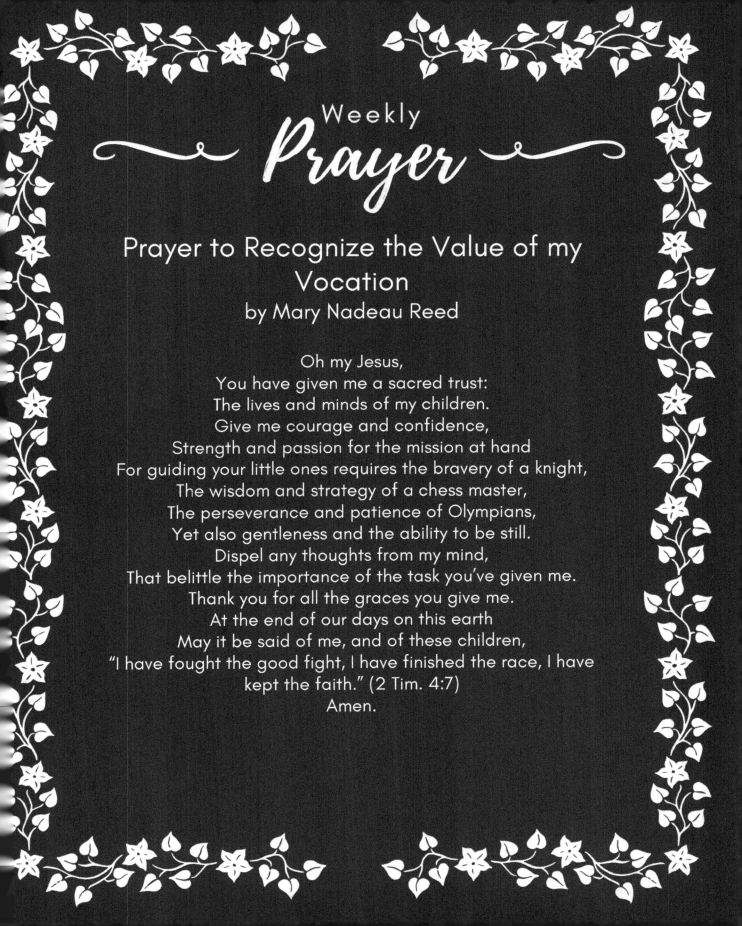

Weekly
Prayer

Prayer to Recognize the Value of my Vocation
by Mary Nadeau Reed

Oh my Jesus,
You have given me a sacred trust:
The lives and minds of my children.
Give me courage and confidence,
Strength and passion for the mission at hand
For guiding your little ones requires the bravery of a knight,
The wisdom and strategy of a chess master,
The perseverance and patience of Olympians,
Yet also gentleness and the ability to be still.
Dispel any thoughts from my mind,
That belittle the importance of the task you've given me.
Thank you for all the graces you give me.
At the end of our days on this earth
May it be said of me, and of these children,
"I have fought the good fight, I have finished the race, I have
kept the faith." (2 Tim. 4:7)
Amen.

Prayer Goals

Prayer Intentions

For whom or what do I want to pray this week? Anyone who frustrates me, or has caused harm to myself or those I love. Anyone/anything who has touched my heart.

"Not all of us can do great things. But we can do *small things with great love.*"
-Mother Teresa of Calcutta

My "small things" this week:

Checklist

We draw a box next to any goals we want to make for ourselves this week, and check them off as we go.

Morning Offering

Evening Prayer or Liturgy of the Hours

Daily/Weekly Rosary

Angelus

Scripture Reading

Divine Mercy Chaplet

Other: _____

Weekday/Daily Mass

Confession

Fasting

Read a Saint Biography

Give alms or a donation

Novena

Volunteer at Homeless Shelter or Food Bank
(or other Corporal Work of Mercy)

first, Breathe

Breathe in ...
7 seconds.
Hold your breath ...
7 seconds.
Breathe out ...
7 seconds.

Repeat.

As many times
as you like.

second, Become aware of God's Presence

third, Thanksgiving

Lord, I realize that all, even myself, is a gift from you. Today, for what things am I most grateful?

fourth, Reflect

Romans 8:26

"An arrow must be pulled back before being propelled forward."
– Anonymous

fifth, Examination

Lord, open my eyes and ears to be more honest with myself. Show me what has been happening to me and in me this day. Today, how have I experienced your love?

_____
_____
_____
_____
_____
_____
_____
_____
_____
_____
_____
_____
_____
_____

sixth Contrition

Today, what choices have been inadequate responses to your love?

_____
_____
_____
_____
_____
_____
_____

seventh, Hope

Lord, let me look with longing toward the future. How will I let you lead me to a brighter tomorrow?

_____
_____
_____
_____
_____
_____
_____

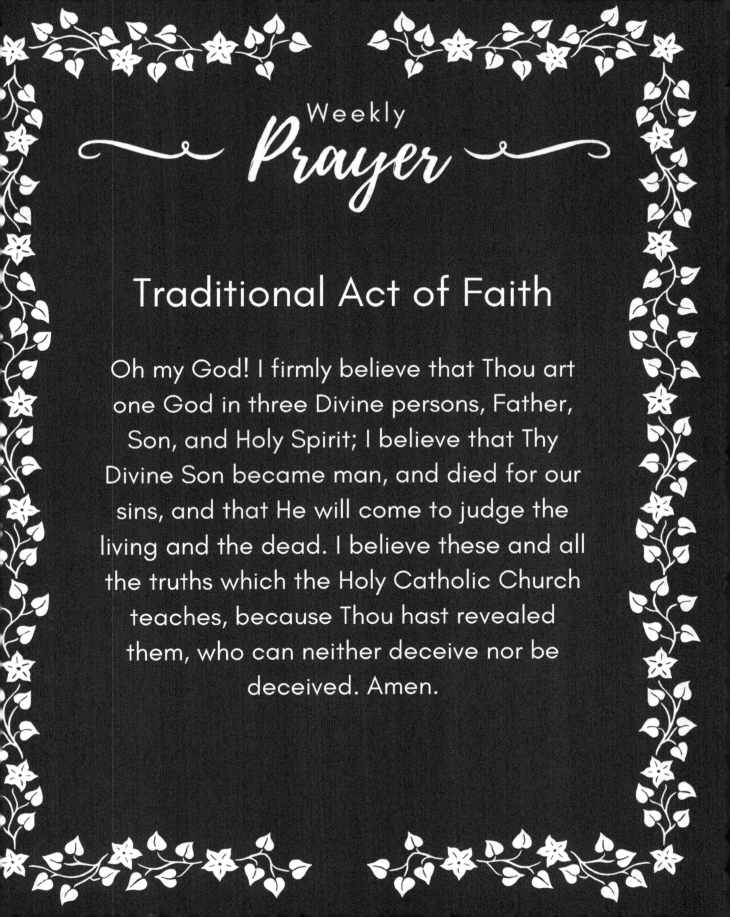

Weekly *Prayer*

Traditional Act of Faith

Oh my God! I firmly believe that Thou art one God in three Divine persons, Father, Son, and Holy Spirit; I believe that Thy Divine Son became man, and died for our sins, and that He will come to judge the living and the dead. I believe these and all the truths which the Holy Catholic Church teaches, because Thou hast revealed them, who can neither deceive nor be deceived. Amen.

Prayer Goals

Prayer Intentions

For whom or what do I want to pray this week? Anyone who frustrates me, or has caused harm to myself or those I love. Anyone/anything who has touched my heart.

_____
_____
_____
_____
_____
_____
_____
_____

"Not all of us can do great things. But we can do *small things with great love.*"
-Mother Teresa of Calcutta

My "small things" this week:

_____
_____
_____
_____
_____
_____
_____
_____
_____
_____

Checklist

We draw a box next to any goals we want to make for ourselves this week, and check them off as we go.

Morning Offering

Evening Prayer or Liturgy of the Hours

Daily/Weekly Rosary

Angelus

Scripture Reading

Divine Mercy Chaplet

Other: _____

Weekday/Daily Mass

Confession

Fasting

Read a Saint Biography

Give alms or a donation

Novena

Volunteer at Homeless Shelter or Food Bank
(or other Corporal Work of Mercy)

first,
Breathe

Week Twenty-Six

third,
Thanksgiving

Lord, I realize that all, even myself, is a gift from you. Today, for what things am I most grateful?

Breathe in ...
7 seconds.
Hold your breath ...
7 seconds.
Breathe out ...
7 seconds.

Repeat.

As many times as you like.

second,
Become aware of
God's Presence

fourth,
Reflect

Philippians 4:6-7

"Let nothing disturb you, let nothing frighten you. All things are passing away. But God never changes. Patience obtains all things. Whoever has God lacks nothing; God alone suffices."
-St. Teresa of Avila

fifth,
Examination

Lord, open my eyes and ears to be more honest with myself. Show me what has been happening to me and in me this day. Today, how have I experienced your love?

_____
_____
_____
_____
_____
_____
_____
_____
_____
_____
_____

sixth
Contrition

Today, what choices have been inadequate responses to your love?

_____
_____
_____
_____
_____
_____

seventh,
Hope

Lord, let me look with longing toward the future. How will I let you lead me to a brighter tomorrow?

_____
_____
_____
_____
_____
_____

Weekly
Prayer

Serenity Prayer

God, grant me the serenity
to accept the things I cannot change,
the courage to change the things I can,
and the wisdom to know the difference.
Living one day at a time,
enjoying one moment at a time;
accepting hardship as a pathway to peace;
taking, as Jesus did,
this sinful world as it is,
not as I would have it;
trusting that You will make all things right
if I surrender to Your will;
so that I may be reasonably happy in this life
and supremely happy with You
forever in the next.
Amen.

Prayer Goals

Prayer Intentions

For whom or what do I want to pray this week? Anyone who frustrates me, or has caused harm to myself or those I love. Anyone/anything who has touched my heart.

_____
_____
_____
_____
_____
_____
_____

"Not all of us can do great things. But we can do *small things with great love.*"

-Mother Teresa of Calcutta

My "small things" this week:

_____
_____
_____

Checklist

We draw a box next to any goals we want to make for ourselves this week, and check them off as we go.

_____
_____
_____
_____
_____
_____
_____

Morning Offering

Evening Prayer or Liturgy of the Hours

Daily/Weekly Rosary

Angelus

Scripture Reading

Divine Mercy Chaplet

Other: _____

Weekday/Daily Mass

Confession

Fasting

Read a Saint Biography

Give alms or a donation

Novena

Volunteer at Homeless Shelter or Food Bank
(or other Corporal Work of Mercy)

Week Twenty-Seven

first, Breathe

Breathe in ...
7 seconds.
Hold your breath ...
7 seconds.
Breathe out ...
7 seconds.

Repeat.

As many times
as you like.

second, Become aware of God's Presence

third, Thanksgiving

Lord, I realize that all, even myself, is a gift from you. Today, for what things am I most grateful?

fourth,
Reflect

Thessalonians 2:16-17

"Aim at Heaven and you will get Earth 'thrown in':
aim at Earth and you will get neither." - C.S. Lewis

fifth,
Examination

Lord, open my eyes and ears to be more honest with myself. Show me what has been happening to me and in me this day. Today, how have I experienced your love?

_____
_____
_____
_____
_____
_____
_____
_____
_____
_____

sixth
Contrition

Today, what choices have been inadequate responses to your love?

_____
_____
_____
_____
_____
_____
_____

seventh,
Hope

Lord, let me look with longing toward the future. How will I let you lead me to a brighter tomorrow?

_____
_____
_____
_____
_____
_____
_____

Weekly
Prayer

Prayer to Communicate
Who the Lord is to my Children
by Mary Nadeau Reed

Lord,
Give me balance.
As I speak with my children,
Through my words, through my actions,
May it be You they hear and see.

May everything I say and that I do
Give glory to your Name.

Help me to keep my eyes on you,
My perspective in focus.
You want these children to have fruitful lives even more than I
do,
Lives that touch others,
that show forth your power and your goodness.

Please come fill my words, and open their ears to hear you.
Nothing more and nothing less. Only you.
And help me to remember that this life is "our ship and not our
home." (-St. Therese of Lisieux)
Amen.

Prayer Goals

Prayer Intentions

For whom or what do I want to pray this week? Anyone who frustrates me, or has caused harm to myself or those I love. Anyone/anything who has touched my heart.

_____

_____

_____

_____

_____

_____

_____

> "Not all of us can do great things. But we can do
>
> *small things with great love.*"
>
> —Mother Teresa of Calcutta

My "small things" this week:

_____

_____

_____

_____

_____

_____

_____

_____

_____

_____

_____

_____

_____

Checklist

We draw a box next to any goals we want to make for ourselves this week, and check them off as we go.

Morning Offering

Evening Prayer or Liturgy of the Hours

Daily/Weekly Rosary

Angelus

Scripture Reading

Divine Mercy Chaplet

Other: _____

Weekday/Daily Mass

Confession

Fasting

Read a Saint Biography

Give alms or a donation

Novena

Volunteer at Homeless Shelter or Food Bank
(or other Corporal Work of Mercy)

first, Breathe

Breathe in ...
7 seconds.
Hold your breath ...
7 seconds.
Breathe out ...
7 seconds.

Repeat.

As many times
as you like.

second, Become aware of God's Presence

third, Thanksgiving

Lord, I realize that all, even myself, is a gift from you. Today, for what things am I most grateful?

fourth, Reflect

Matthew 11:28-30

"The past to mercy, the present to grace, the future to Providence ... Let us ask for grace ... each morning grace permits us ... to make it again to the evening.
–Servant of God Chiara Corbella Petrillo, *A Witness to Joy*

fifth, Examination

Lord, open my eyes and ears to be more honest with myself. Show me what has been happening to me and in me this day. Today, how have I experienced your love?

_____
_____
_____
_____
_____
_____
_____
_____
_____
_____
_____

sixth Contrition

Today, what choices have been inadequate responses to your love?

_____
_____
_____
_____
_____
_____
_____

seventh, Hope

Lord, let me look with longing toward the future. How will I let you lead me to a brighter tomorrow?

_____
_____
_____
_____
_____
_____
_____

Weekly *Prayer*

Prayer of Praise for God's Victory from Psalm 108

My heart is steadfast, O God,
My heart is steadfast!
I will sing and make melody!
Awake, my soul!
Awake, O harp and lyre!
I will awake the dawn!
I will give thanks to Thee,
O Lord, among the peoples,
I will sing praises to Thee among the nations.
For Thy steadfast love
is great above the heavens,
Thy faithfulness reaches to the clouds.
Amen.

Prayer Goals

Prayer Intentions

For whom or what do I want to pray this week? Anyone who frustrates me, or has caused harm to myself or those I love. Anyone/anything who has touched my heart.

_____
_____
_____
_____
_____
_____
_____
_____

> "Not all of us can do great things. But we can do _small things with great love._"
> —Mother Teresa of Calcutta

My "small things" this week:

_____
_____
_____
_____
_____
_____
_____
_____
_____
_____
_____

Checklist

We draw a box next to any goals we want to make for ourselves this week, and check them off as we go.

Morning Offering

Evening Prayer or Liturgy of the Hours

Daily/Weekly Rosary

Angelus

Scripture Reading

Divine Mercy Chaplet

Other: _____

Weekday/Daily Mass

Confession

Fasting

Read a Saint Biography

Give alms or a donation

Novena

Volunteer at Homeless Shelter or Food Bank
(or other Corporal Work of Mercy)

first, Breathe

Breathe in ...
7 seconds.
Hold your breath ...
7 seconds.
Breathe out ...
7 seconds.

Repeat.

As many times
as you like.

second, Become aware of God's Presence

third, Thanksgiving

Lord, I realize that all, even myself, is a gift from you. Today, for what things am I most grateful?

fourth,
Reflect

Romans 8:28

"And of what should we be afraid? Our captain on this battlefield is Christ Jesus. We have discovered what we have to do. Christ has bound our enemies for us and weakened them that they cannot overcome us unless we so choose to let them. So we must fight courageously..."
– St. Catherine of Siena

fifth,
Examination

Lord, open my eyes and ears to be more honest with myself. Show me what has been happening to me and in me this day. Today, how have I experienced your love?

_____
_____
_____
_____
_____
_____
_____
_____
_____
_____
_____
_____

sixth
Contrition

Today, what choices have been inadequate responses to your love?

_____
_____
_____
_____
_____

seventh,
Hope

Lord, let me look with longing toward the future. How will I let you lead me to a brighter tomorrow?

_____
_____
_____
_____
_____

Weekly
Prayer

Prayer for Direction
by Mary Nadeau Reed

Dear Lord,
Give me the grace to quiet my heart,
To silence the chatter in my mind,
To listen for the clarity and peace that only you give.
Help me to take good counsel from those in my life,
To disregard any paths that are not of you.
May our lives and the choices we make give you glory.

Lord, we know that you can take even
our greatest mistakes,
And bring beauty from the ashes.
Help me to make the best decision I can,
And when I have done that,
I entrust all to your kind and merciful Providence.
Amen.

Prayer Goals

Prayer Intentions

For whom or what do I want to pray this week? Anyone who frustrates me, or has caused harm to myself or those I love. Anyone/anything who has touched my heart.

_____
_____
_____
_____
_____
_____
_____
_____

> "Not all of us can do great things. But we can do
> *small things with great love.*"
> -Mother Teresa of Calcutta

My "small things" this week:

_____
_____
_____
_____
_____
_____
_____
_____
_____
_____
_____
_____

Checklist

We draw a box next to any goals we want to make for ourselves this week, and check them off as we go.

Morning Offering

Evening Prayer or Liturgy of the Hours

Daily/Weekly Rosary

Angelus

Scripture Reading

Divine Mercy Chaplet

Other: _____

Weekday/Daily Mass

Confession

Fasting

Read a Saint Biography

Give alms or a donation

Novena

Volunteer at Homeless Shelter or Food Bank
(or other Corporal Work of Mercy)

first, Breathe

Breathe in ...
7 seconds.
Hold your breath ...
7 seconds.
Breathe out ...
7 seconds.

Repeat.

As many times
as you like.

second, Become aware of God's Presence

third, Thanksgiving

Lord, I realize that all, even myself, is a gift from you. Today, for what things am I most grateful?

fourth,
Reflect

3 John 1:4

"Our greatest task then is to put living ideas in front of our children like a feast. We've been charged to cultivate the souls of our children, to nourish them in truth, goodness, and beauty, to raise them up in wisdom and eloquence. It is to those ends that we labor."
-Sarah Mackenzie

fifth,
Examination

Lord, open my eyes and ears to be more honest with myself. Show me what has been happening to me and in me this day. Today, how have I experienced your love?

_____
_____
_____
_____
_____
_____
_____
_____
_____

sixth
Contrition

Today, what choices have been inadequate responses to your love?

seventh,
Hope

Lord, let me look with longing toward the future. How will I let you lead me to a brighter tomorrow?

_____   _____
_____   _____
_____   _____
_____   _____
_____   _____
_____   _____
_____   _____

Weekly
Prayer

Prayer to Show
Our Children Who God Is
by Mary Nadeau Reed

Lord Jesus,
You have given me stewardship of the most valuable
gift in the universe,
The souls of Your children.
They watch everything I do.
They listen to the words I say.
May all that I am communicate Your Truth, Your
Beauty, Your Goodness.

Joy is found in You. Life is found in You.
Nothing is more important than sharing who
You are with my family.
May I always communicate that
which is true, good and beautiful
To the little ones You've entrusted to my care.
And when I fail, when I am all too human,
In those moments may I all the more demonstrate
how good and merciful You are.
Amen.

Prayer Goals

Prayer Intentions

For whom or what do I want to pray this week? Anyone who frustrates me, or has caused harm to myself or those I love. Anyone/anything who has touched my heart.

_____
_____
_____
_____
_____
_____
_____

> "Not all of us can do great things. But we can do *small things with great love.*"
> —Mother Teresa of Calcutta
>
> My "small things" this week:

_____
_____
_____

Checklist

We draw a box next to any goals we want to make for ourselves this week, and check them off as we go.

Morning Offering

Evening Prayer or Liturgy of the Hours

Daily/Weekly Rosary

Angelus

Scripture Reading

Divine Mercy Chaplet

Other: _____

Weekday/Daily Mass

Confession

Fasting

Read a Saint Biography

Give alms or a donation

Novena

Volunteer at Homeless Shelter or Food Bank
(or other Corporal Work of Mercy)

_____
_____
_____
_____
_____
_____
_____

first,
Breathe

Breathe in ...
7 seconds.
Hold your breath ...
7 seconds.
Breathe out ...
7 seconds.

Repeat.

As many times
as you like.

second,
Become aware of
God's Presence

third,
Thanksgiving

Lord, I realize that all, even myself, is a gift from you. Today, for what things am I most grateful?

fourth,
Reflect

Deuteronomy 16:15

"The real problem of the Christian life comes where people do not usually look for it. It comes the very moment you wake up each morning. All your wishes and hopes for the day rush at you like wild animals. And the first job each morning consists simply in shoving them all back; and listening to that other voice, taking that other point of view, letting that other larger, stronger, quieter life come flowing in. And so on, all day. Standing back from all your natural fussings and frettings; coming in and out of the wind." – C.S. Lewis, *Mere Christianity*

fifth,
Examination

Lord, open my eyes and ears to be more honest with myself. Show me what has been happening to me and in me this day. Today, how have I experienced your love?

_____
_____
_____
_____
_____
_____
_____
_____
_____
_____

sixth
Contrition

Today, what choices have been inadequate responses to your love?

_____
_____
_____
_____
_____

seventh,
Hope

Lord, let me look with longing toward the future. How will I let you lead me to a brighter tomorrow?

_____
_____
_____
_____
_____

Weekly
Prayer

The Lord's Prayer
(Try praying this familiar prayer slower
than you usually do. Line by line.)

Our Father, who art in heaven,
hallowed be Thy name.
Thy kingdom come;
Thy will be done on earth as it is in heaven.
Give us this day our daily bread;
and forgive us our trespasses as we
forgive those who trespass against us;
and lead us not into temptation, but deliver us
from evil.
Amen.

Prayer Goals

Prayer Intentions

For whom or what do I want to pray this week? Anyone who frustrates me, or has caused harm to myself or those I love. Anyone/anything who has touched my heart.

_____
_____
_____
_____
_____
_____

"Not all of us can do great things. But we can do *small things with great love.*"
-Mother Teresa of Calcutta

My "small things" this week:

_____
_____
_____
_____
_____
_____
_____
_____
_____
_____

Checklist

We draw a box next to any goals we want to make for ourselves this week, and check them off as we go.

Morning Offering

Evening Prayer or Liturgy of the Hours

Daily/Weekly Rosary

Angelus

Scripture Reading

Divine Mercy Chaplet

Other: _____

Weekday/Daily Mass

Confession

Fasting

Read a Saint Biography

Give alms or a donation

Novena

Volunteer at Homeless Shelter or Food Bank
(or other Corporal Work of Mercy)

first, *Breathe*

Breathe in ...
7 seconds.
Hold your breath ...
7 seconds.
Breathe out ...
7 seconds.

Repeat.

As many times
as you like.

second, Become aware of *God's Presence*

third, *Thanksgiving*

Lord, I realize that all, even myself, is a gift from you. Today, for what things am I most grateful?

fourth,
Reflect

Galatians 6:9

"Jesus, help me to simplify my life by learning what you want me to be and becoming that person." – St. Thérèse of Lisieux

fifth,
Examination

Lord, open my eyes and ears to be more honest with myself. Show me what has been happening to me and in me this day. Today, how have I experienced your love?

_____
_____
_____
_____
_____
_____
_____
_____
_____
_____
_____
_____

sixth
Contrition

Today, what choices have been inadequate responses to your love?

_____
_____
_____
_____
_____
_____

seventh,
Hope

Lord, let me look with longing toward the future. How will I let you lead me to a brighter tomorrow?

_____
_____
_____
_____
_____
_____

Weekly Prayer

Litany of Trust, Part One
From the Sisters of Life

From the belief that I have to earn Your love,
Deliver me, Jesus.
From the fear that I am unlovable,
Deliver me, Jesus.
From the false security that I have what it takes,
Deliver me, Jesus.
From the fear that trusting You will leave me more destitute,
Deliver me, Jesus.
From all suspicion of Your words and promises,
Deliver me, Jesus.
From the rebellion against childlike dependency on You,
Deliver me, Jesus.
From refusals and reluctances in accepting Your will,
Deliver me, Jesus.
From anxiety about the future,
Deliver me, Jesus.
From resentment or excessive preoccupation with the past,
Deliver me, Jesus.
From restless self-seeking in the present moment,
Deliver me, Jesus.
From disbelief in Your love and presence,
Deliver me, Jesus.
From the fear of being asked to give more than I have,
Deliver me, Jesus.
From the belief that my life has no meaning or worth,
Deliver me, Jesus.
From the fear of what love demands,
Deliver me, Jesus.
From discouragement,
Deliver me, Jesus.

Prayer Goals

Prayer Intentions

For whom or what do I want to pray this week? Anyone who frustrates me, or has caused harm to myself or those I love. Anyone/anything who has touched my heart.

"Not all of us can do great things. But we can do *small things with great love.*"
-Mother Teresa of Calcutta

My "small things" this week:

Checklist

We draw a box next to any goals we want to make for ourselves this week, and check them off as we go.

- Morning Offering
- Evening Prayer or Liturgy of the Hours
- Daily/Weekly Rosary
- Angelus
- Scripture Reading
- Divine Mercy Chaplet
- Other: _____

- Weekday/Daily Mass
- Confession
- Fasting
- Read a Saint Biography
- Give alms or a donation
- Novena
- Volunteer at Homeless Shelter or Food Bank (or other Corporal Work of Mercy)

first,
Breathe

Breathe in ...
7 seconds.
Hold your breath ...
7 seconds.
Breathe out ...
7 seconds.

Repeat.

As many times
as you like.

second,
Become aware of
God's Presence

third,
Thanksgiving

Lord, I realize that all, even myself, is a gift from you. Today, for what things am I most grateful?

137

fourth, Reflect

Colossians 3:23

"Parents have the first responsibility for the education of their children. They bear witness to this responsibility by creating a home where tenderness, forgiveness, respect, fidelity, and disinterested service are the rule.
–The Catechism of the Catholic Church #2223

fifth, Examination

Lord, open my eyes and ears to be more honest with myself. Show me what has been happening to me and in me this day. Today, how have I experienced your love?

_____
_____
_____
_____
_____
_____
_____
_____
_____

_____
_____
_____
_____
_____
_____
_____
_____
_____

sixth, Contrition

Today, what choices have been inadequate responses to your love?

_____
_____
_____
_____
_____
_____

seventh, Hope

Lord, let me look with longing toward the future. How will I let you lead me to a brighter tomorrow?

_____
_____
_____
_____
_____
_____

Weekly *Prayer*

Litany of Trust, Part Two
From the Sisters of Life

That You are continually holding me, sustaining me, loving me,
Jesus, I trust in You.
That Your love goes deeper than my sins and failings and transforms me,
Jesus, I trust in You.
That not knowing what tomorrow brings is an invitation to lean on You,
Jesus, I trust in You.
That You are with me in my suffering,
Jesus, I trust in You.
That my suffering, united to Your own, will bear fruit in this life and the next,
Jesus, I trust in You.
That You will not leave me orphan, that You are present in Your Church,
Jesus, I trust in You.
That Your plan is better than anything else,
Jesus, I trust in You.
That You always hear me and in Your goodness, always respond to me
Jesus, I trust in You.
That You give me the grace to accept forgiveness and to forgive others
Jesus, I trust in You.
That You give me all the strength I need for what is asked
Jesus, I trust in You.
That my life is a gift,
Jesus, I trust in You.
That You will teach me to trust You,
Jesus, I trust in You.
That You are my Lord and my God,
Jesus, I trust in You.
That I am Your beloved one,
Jesus, I trust in You.

Prayer Goals

Prayer Intentions

For whom or what do I want to pray this week? Anyone who frustrates me, or has caused harm to myself or those I love. Anyone/anything who has touched my heart.

_____
_____
_____
_____
_____
_____
_____
_____

"Not all of us can do great things. But we can do

small things with great love."

-Mother Teresa of Calcutta

My "small things" this week:

_____
_____

Checklist

We draw a box next to any goals we want to make for ourselves this week, and check them off as we go.

_____
_____
_____
_____
_____
_____
_____
_____
_____
_____

Morning Offering

Evening Prayer or Liturgy of the Hours

Daily/Weekly Rosary

Angelus

Scripture Reading

Divine Mercy Chaplet

Other: _____

Weekday/Daily Mass

Confession

Fasting

Read a Saint Biography

Give alms or a donation

Novena

Volunteer at Homeless Shelter or Food Bank
(or other Corporal Work of Mercy)

first, Breathe

Breathe in ...
7 seconds.
Hold your breath ...
7 seconds.
Breathe out ...
7 seconds.

Repeat.

As many times
as you like.

second, Become aware of God's Presence

third, Thanksgiving

Lord, I realize that all, even myself, is a gift from you. Today, for what things am I most grateful?

fourth, Reflect

Psalm 127:1

"What really matters in life is that we are loved by Christ and that we love Him in return. In comparison to the love of Jesus, everything else is secondary. And, without the love of Jesus, everything is useless." – St. Pope John Paul II

fifth, Examination

Lord, open my eyes and ears to be more honest with myself. Show me what has been happening to me and in me this day. Today, how have I experienced your love?

_____ _____
_____ _____
_____ _____
_____ _____
_____ _____
_____ _____
_____ _____
_____ _____
_____ _____

sixth, Contrition

Today, what choices have been inadequate responses to your love?

_____
_____
_____
_____
_____
_____

seventh, Hope

Lord, let me look with longing toward the future. How will I let you lead me to a brighter tomorrow?

_____
_____
_____
_____
_____
_____

Weekly
Prayer

Prayer for Our Families from Ephesians 3

I bow my knees before the Father, from whom every family in heaven and on earth is named, that according to the riches of His glory He may grant you to be strengthened with might through His Spirit in the inner man, and that Christ may dwell in your hearts through faith; that you, being rooted and grounded in love, may have power to comprehend with all the saints what is the breadth and length and height and depth, and to know the love of Christ which surpasses knowledge, that you may be filled with all the fullness of God. Now to him who by the power at work within us is able to do far more abundantly than all that we ask or think, to him be glory in the church and in Christ Jesus through all generations, for ever and ever. Amen.

Prayer Goals

Prayer Intentions

For whom or what do I want to pray this week? Anyone who frustrates me, or has caused harm to myself or those I love. Anyone/anything who has touched my heart.

_____
_____
_____
_____
_____
_____

> "Not all of us can do great things. But we can do _small things with great love._"
> —Mother Teresa of Calcutta

My "small things" this week:

_____
_____
_____
_____
_____
_____
_____
_____
_____
_____

Checklist

We draw a box next to any goals we want to make for ourselves this week, and check them off as we go.

Morning Offering

Evening Prayer or Liturgy of the Hours

Daily/Weekly Rosary

Angelus

Scripture Reading

Divine Mercy Chaplet

Other: _____

Weekday/Daily Mass

Confession

Fasting

Read a Saint Biography

Give alms or a donation

Novena

Volunteer at Homeless Shelter or Food Bank
(or other Corporal Work of Mercy)

first, Breathe

Breathe in ...
7 seconds.
Hold your breath ...
7 seconds.
Breathe out ...
7 seconds.

Repeat.

As many times
as you like.

second, Become aware of God's Presence

third, Thanksgiving

Lord, I realize that all, even myself, is a gift from you. Today, for what things am I most grateful?

fourth, Reflect

Matthew 5:16

"Nothing is so contagious as example."
–François de la Rochefoucauld

fifth, Examination

Lord, open my eyes and ears to be more honest with myself. Show me what has been happening to me and in me this day. Today, how have I experienced your love?

_____

_____

_____

_____

_____

_____

_____

_____

_____

_____

_____

_____

sixth Contrition

Today, what choices have been inadequate responses to your love?

_____

_____

_____

_____

_____

_____

seventh, Hope

Lord, let me look with longing toward the future. How will I let you lead me to a brighter tomorrow?

_____

_____

_____

_____

_____

_____

Weekly *Prayer*

Prayer to Teach My Children in the Everyday Moments
by Mary Nadeau Reed

Dear Jesus,
I try so hard.
I agonize over which activities and programs
are best for my children.
I overlook the ordinary moments of ordinary days,
When they are learning so much more than I realize.

Help me to remember that you are teaching them in it all.
As we do laundry together, as we cook and eat,
As we read books, and explore our backyard.
Help me to never underestimate the value of those hours and
those minutes.

I ask you to take my humble offering and transform it,
Into a nourishing banquet for these precious little ones.
I ask you to elevate and fill our daily rhythms,
So in the ordinary and the beautiful moments of our lives,
May these children find meaning.
May they find communion with you.
Amen.

Prayer Goals

Prayer Intentions

For whom or what do I want to pray this week? Anyone who frustrates me, or has caused harm to myself or those I love. Anyone/anything who has touched my heart.

> "Not all of us can do great things. But we can do *small things with great love."*
> -Mother Teresa of Calcutta

My "small things" this week:

Checklist

We draw a box next to any goals we want to make for ourselves this week, and check them off as we go.

Morning Offering

Evening Prayer or Liturgy of the Hours

Daily/Weekly Rosary

Angelus

Scripture Reading

Divine Mercy Chaplet

Other: _____

Weekday/Daily Mass

Confession

Fasting

Read a Saint Biography

Give alms or a donation

Novena

Volunteer at Homeless Shelter or Food Bank
(or other Corporal Work of Mercy)

first,
Breathe

Breathe in ...
7 seconds.
Hold your breath ...
7 seconds.
Breathe out ...
7 seconds.

Repeat.

As many times
as you like.

second,
Become aware of
God's Presence

third,
Thanksgiving

Lord, I realize that all, even myself, is a gift from you. Today, for what things am I most grateful?

fourth,
Reflect

Psalm 3:5-6

"The stillness of prayer is the most essential condition for fruitful action.
Before all else, the disciple kneels down."
– St. Gianna Beretta Molla

fifth,
Examination

Lord, open my eyes and ears to be more honest with myself. Show me what has been happening to me and in me this day. Today, how have I experienced your love?

_____
_____
_____
_____
_____
_____
_____
_____
_____
_____

sixth
Contrition

Today, what choices have been inadequate responses to your love?

_____
_____
_____
_____
_____

seventh,
Hope

Lord, let me look with longing toward the future. How will I let you lead me to a brighter tomorrow?

_____
_____
_____
_____
_____

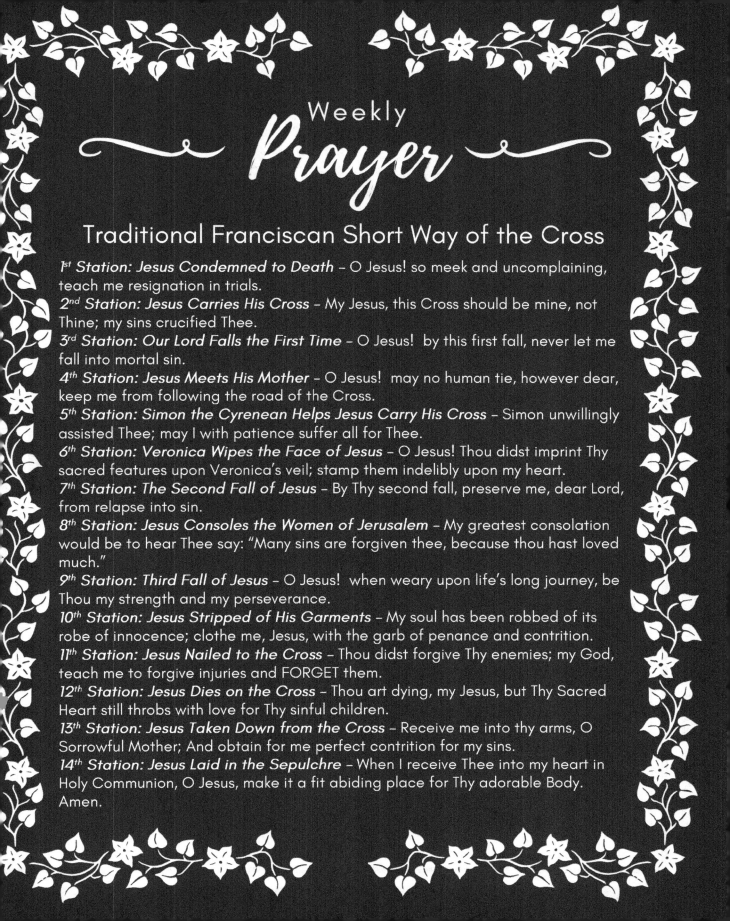

Weekly *Prayer*

Traditional Franciscan Short Way of the Cross

1st Station: Jesus Condemned to Death – O Jesus! so meek and uncomplaining, teach me resignation in trials.

2nd Station: Jesus Carries His Cross – My Jesus, this Cross should be mine, not Thine; my sins crucified Thee.

3rd Station: Our Lord Falls the First Time – O Jesus! by this first fall, never let me fall into mortal sin.

4th Station: Jesus Meets His Mother – O Jesus! may no human tie, however dear, keep me from following the road of the Cross.

5th Station: Simon the Cyrenean Helps Jesus Carry His Cross – Simon unwillingly assisted Thee; may I with patience suffer all for Thee.

6th Station: Veronica Wipes the Face of Jesus – O Jesus! Thou didst imprint Thy sacred features upon Veronica's veil; stamp them indelibly upon my heart.

7th Station: The Second Fall of Jesus – By Thy second fall, preserve me, dear Lord, from relapse into sin.

8th Station: Jesus Consoles the Women of Jerusalem – My greatest consolation would be to hear Thee say: "Many sins are forgiven thee, because thou hast loved much."

9th Station: Third Fall of Jesus – O Jesus! when weary upon life's long journey, be Thou my strength and my perseverance.

10th Station: Jesus Stripped of His Garments – My soul has been robbed of its robe of innocence; clothe me, Jesus, with the garb of penance and contrition.

11th Station: Jesus Nailed to the Cross – Thou didst forgive Thy enemies; my God, teach me to forgive injuries and FORGET them.

12th Station: Jesus Dies on the Cross – Thou art dying, my Jesus, but Thy Sacred Heart still throbs with love for Thy sinful children.

13th Station: Jesus Taken Down from the Cross – Receive me into thy arms, O Sorrowful Mother; And obtain for me perfect contrition for my sins.

14th Station: Jesus Laid in the Sepulchre – When I receive Thee into my heart in Holy Communion, O Jesus, make it a fit abiding place for Thy adorable Body. Amen.

Prayer Goals

Prayer Intentions

For whom or what do I want to pray this week? Anyone who frustrates me, or has caused harm to myself or those I love. Anyone/anything who has touched my heart.

_____
_____
_____
_____
_____
_____
_____

"Not all of us can do great things. But we can do *small things with great love.*"

-Mother Teresa of Calcutta

My "small things" this week:

_____
_____
_____

Checklist

We draw a box next to any goals we want to make for ourselves this week, and check them off as we go.

_____
_____
_____
_____
_____
_____
_____
_____
_____

Morning Offering

Evening Prayer or Liturgy of the Hours

Daily/Weekly Rosary

Angelus

Scripture Reading

Divine Mercy Chaplet

Other: _____

Weekday/Daily Mass

Confession

Fasting

Read a Saint Biography

Give alms or a donation

Novena

Volunteer at Homeless Shelter or Food Bank
(or other Corporal Work of Mercy)

first, *Breathe*

Breathe in ...
7 seconds.
Hold your breath ...
7 seconds.
Breathe out ...
7 seconds.

Repeat.

As many times
as you like.

second, Become aware of *God's Presence*

third, *Thanksgiving*

Lord, I realize that all, even myself, is a gift from you. Today, for what things am I most grateful?

fourth,
Reflect

Jeremiah 29:11

"Let us love, since that is what our hearts were made for."
–St. Therese of Lisieux

fifth,
Examination

Lord, open my eyes and ears to be more honest with myself. Show me what has been happening to me and in me this day. Today, how have I experienced your love?

_____
_____
_____
_____
_____
_____
_____
_____
_____
_____
_____

sixth
Contrition

Today, what choices have been inadequate responses to your love?

_____
_____
_____
_____
_____
_____
_____

seventh,
Hope

Lord, let me look with longing toward the future. How will I let you lead me to a brighter tomorrow?

_____
_____
_____
_____
_____
_____
_____

Weekly
Prayer

Traditional Act of Charity

Oh my God! I love Thee above all things, with my whole heart and soul, because Thou art all-good and worthy of all love. I love my neighbor as myself for the love of Thee. I forgive all who have injured me, and ask pardon of all whom I have injured. Amen.

Prayer Goals

Prayer Intentions

For whom or what do I want to pray this week? Anyone who frustrates me, or has caused harm to myself or those I love. Anyone/anything who has touched my heart.

_____
_____
_____
_____
_____
_____
_____
_____

"Not all of us can do great things. But we can do *small things with great love.*"
-Mother Teresa of Calcutta

My "small things" this week:

_____
_____
_____
_____
_____
_____
_____
_____
_____
_____
_____

Checklist

We draw a box next to any goals we want to make for ourselves this week, and check them off as we go.

Morning Offering

Evening Prayer or Liturgy of the Hours

Daily/Weekly Rosary

Angelus

Scripture Reading

Divine Mercy Chaplet

Other: _____

Weekday/Daily Mass

Confession

Fasting

Read a Saint Biography

Give alms or a donation

Novena

Volunteer at Homeless Shelter or Food Bank
(or other Corporal Work of Mercy)

first, Breathe

Breathe in ...
7 seconds.
Hold your breath ...
7 seconds.
Breathe out ...
7 seconds.

Repeat.

As many times
as you like.

second, Become aware of God's Presence

third, Thanksgiving

Lord, I realize that all, even myself, is a gift from you. Today, for what things am I most grateful?

fourth, Reflect

Colossians 3:14-15

"Not all of us can do great things.
But we can do small things with great love."
- St. Teresa of Calcutta

fifth, Examination

Lord, open my eyes and ears to be more honest with myself. Show me what has been happening to me and in me this day. Today, how have I experienced your love?

_____   _____
_____   _____
_____   _____
_____   _____
_____   _____
_____   _____
_____   _____
_____   _____

sixth Contrition

Today, what choices have been inadequate responses to your love?

_____
_____
_____
_____
_____

seventh, Hope

Lord, let me look with longing toward the future. How will I let you lead me to a brighter tomorrow?

_____
_____
_____
_____
_____

Weekly *Prayer*

Prayer from Psalm 27

The Lord is my light and my salvation;
Whom shall I fear?
The Lord is the stronghold of my life;
Of whom shall I be afraid?...

One thing have I asked of the Lord,
That will I seek after;
That I may dwell in the house of the Lord
All the days of my life,
To behold the beauty of the Lord,
And to inquire in His temple.

Hear, O Lord, when I cry aloud,
Be gracious to me and answer me!
Thou hast said, "Seek ye my face."
My heart says to Thee,
"Thy face, Lord, do I seek."
Hide not Thy face from me...

Teach me thy way, O Lord;
And lead me on a level path..

I believe that I shall see the goodness of the Lord
In the land of the living!
Wait for the Lord;
Be strong, and let your heart take courage;
Yea, wait for the Lord!
Amen.

Prayer Goals

Prayer Intentions

For whom or what do I want to pray this week? Anyone who frustrates me, or has caused harm to myself or those I love. Anyone/anything who has touched my heart.

_____
_____
_____
_____
_____
_____
_____
_____

> "Not all of us can do great things. But we can do *small things with great love.*"
> —Mother Teresa of Calcutta

My "small things" this week:

_____
_____
_____
_____
_____
_____
_____
_____
_____
_____
_____

Checklist

We draw a box next to any goals we want to make for ourselves this week, and check them off as we go.

Morning Offering

Evening Prayer or Liturgy of the Hours

Daily/Weekly Rosary

Angelus

Scripture Reading

Divine Mercy Chaplet

Other: _____

Weekday/Daily Mass

Confession

Fasting

Read a Saint Biography

Give alms or a donation

Novena

Volunteer at Homeless Shelter or Food Bank
(or other Corporal Work of Mercy)

first, Breathe

Breathe in ...
7 seconds.
Hold your breath ...
7 seconds.
Breathe out ...
7 seconds.

Repeat.

As many times
as you like.

second, Become aware of God's Presence

third, Thanksgiving

Lord, I realize that all, even myself, is a gift from you. Today, for what things am I most grateful?

fourth, Reflect

Psalm 131:2

"If satan cannot make us bad, he will make us busy."
– Corrie Ten Boom (Concentration Camp Survivor, Christian Writer/Speaker)

fifth, Examination

Lord, open my eyes and ears to be more honest with myself. Show me what has been happening to me and in me this day. Today, how have I experienced your love?

_____
_____
_____
_____
_____
_____
_____
_____
_____
_____
_____

sixth, Contrition

Today, what choices have been inadequate responses to your love?

_____
_____
_____
_____
_____
_____

seventh, Hope

Lord, let me look with longing toward the future. How will I let you lead me to a brighter tomorrow?

_____
_____
_____
_____
_____
_____

Weekly *Prayer*

Prayer to be Available to my Family
by Mary Nadeau Reed

Dearest Father,
I ask you for the grace to be present and
available to my family.
To not let their childhoods pass me by as I busy
myself with task after task.
Remind me of Your Love and Your goodness
and Your plan for us.
Help me to put everything in its proper place,
To choose what matters,
To say "no" to being the servant of a to-do list,
So that I can be available to Your little ones
today. Amen.

Prayer Goals

Prayer Intentions

For whom or what do I want to pray this week? Anyone who frustrates me, or has caused harm to myself or those I love. Anyone/anything who has touched my heart.

_____
_____
_____
_____
_____
_____
_____
_____

"Not all of us can do great things. But we can do *small things with great love.*"
-Mother Teresa of Calcutta

My "small things" this week:

_____
_____
_____

Checklist

We draw a box next to any goals we want to make for ourselves this week, and check them off as we go.

Morning Offering

Evening Prayer or Liturgy of the Hours

Daily/Weekly Rosary

Angelus

Scripture Reading

Divine Mercy Chaplet

Other: _____

Weekday/Daily Mass

Confession

Fasting

Read a Saint Biography

Give alms or a donation

Novena

Volunteer at Homeless Shelter or Food Bank
(or other Corporal Work of Mercy)

_____
_____
_____
_____
_____
_____
_____
_____
_____
_____

first, *Breathe*

Breathe in ...
7 seconds.
Hold your breath ...
7 seconds.
Breathe out ...
7 seconds.

Repeat.

As many times
as you like.

second, Become aware of *God's Presence*

third, *Thanksgiving*

Lord, I realize that all, even myself, is a gift from you. Today, for what things am I most grateful?

fourth,
Reflect

Proverbs 1:7–8

"Our hearts were made for You, O Lord,
and they are restless until they rest in You."
St. Augustine of Hippo

fifth,
Examination

Lord, open my eyes and ears to be more honest with myself. Show me what has been happening to me and in me this day. Today, how have I experienced your love?

_____
_____
_____
_____
_____
_____
_____
_____
_____

sixth
Contrition

Today, what choices have been inadequate responses to your love?

_____
_____
_____
_____
_____
_____
_____

seventh,
Hope

Lord, let me look with longing toward the future. How will I let you lead me to a brighter tomorrow?

_____
_____
_____
_____
_____
_____
_____

Weekly
Prayer

Anima Christi (Soul of Christ) Prayer

Soul of Christ, sanctify me.
Body of Christ, save me.
Blood of Christ, drench me.
Water from the side of Christ, cleanse me.
Passion of Christ, strengthen me.
O Good Jesus, hear me.
Within your wounds, hide me.
Permit me never to be separated from thee.
From the wicked foe, defend me.
At the hour of my death, call me
And bid me come to thee,
That with thy saints I may praise thee
Forever and ever.
Amen.

Prayer Goals

Prayer Intentions

For whom or what do I want to pray this week? Anyone who frustrates me, or has caused harm to myself or those I love. Anyone/anything who has touched my heart.

_____
_____
_____
_____
_____
_____

"Not all of us can do great things. But we can do *small things with great love.*"
-Mother Teresa of Calcutta

My "small things" this week:

_____
_____
_____
_____
_____
_____
_____
_____
_____

Checklist

We draw a box next to any goals we want to make for ourselves this week, and check them off as we go.

Morning Offering

Evening Prayer or Liturgy of the Hours

Daily/Weekly Rosary

Angelus

Scripture Reading

Divine Mercy Chaplet

Other: _____

Weekday/Daily Mass

Confession

Fasting

Read a Saint Biography

Give alms or a donation

Novena

Volunteer at Homeless Shelter or Food Bank
(or other Corporal Work of Mercy)

first, Breathe

Breathe in ...
7 seconds.
Hold your breath ...
7 seconds.
Breathe out ...
7 seconds.

Repeat.

As many times
as you like.

second, Become aware of God's Presence

third, Thanksgiving

Lord, I realize that all, even myself, is a gift from you. Today, for what things am I most grateful?

fourth,
Reflect

Matthew 6:34

"Faith is to believe what you do not see;
the reward of this faith is to see what you believe."
- St. Augustine

fifth, Examination

Lord, open my eyes and ears to be more honest with myself. Show me what has been happening to me and in me this day. Today, how have I experienced your love?

_____
_____
_____
_____
_____
_____
_____
_____
_____
_____
_____
_____
_____
_____

sixth Contrition

Today, what choices have been inadequate responses to your love?

_____
_____
_____
_____
_____
_____
_____

seventh, Hope

Lord, let me look with longing toward the future. How will I let you lead me to a brighter tomorrow?

_____
_____
_____
_____
_____
_____
_____

Weekly
Prayer

Parent's Prayer in Times of Discouragement
by Mary Nadeau Reed

Dear Lord,
It can feel as though I fail at every turn.

Help me to rest in Your promises.
Help me to remember that it is You who do the work
in my children, and in me.

I give You their time, their education, their lives.
I ask You to guide my words and my actions.
May Your glory shine forth in our days,
Even the messiest ones.
May we always keep our eyes on You.
And may we always seek first Your Kingdom.
Amen.

Prayer Goals

Prayer Intentions

For whom or what do I want to pray this week? Anyone who frustrates me, or has caused harm to myself or those I love. Anyone/anything who has touched my heart.

_____
_____
_____
_____
_____
_____
_____

"Not all of us can do great things. But we can do *small things with great love.*"
-Mother Teresa of Calcutta

My "small things" this week:

_____
_____
_____
_____
_____
_____
_____
_____
_____
_____
_____
_____

Checklist

We draw a box next to any goals we want to make for ourselves this week, and check them off as we go.

Morning Offering

Evening Prayer or Liturgy of the Hours

Daily/Weekly Rosary

Angelus

Scripture Reading

Divine Mercy Chaplet

Other: _____

Weekday/Daily Mass

Confession

Fasting

Read a Saint Biography

Give alms or a donation

Novena

Volunteer at Homeless Shelter or Food Bank
(or other Corporal Work of Mercy)

first,
Breathe

Breathe in ...
7 seconds.
Hold your breath ...
7 seconds.
Breathe out ...
7 seconds.

Repeat.

As many times
as you like.

third,
Thanksgiving

Lord, I realize that all, even myself, is a gift from you. Today, for what things am I most grateful?

second,
Become aware of
God's Presence

fourth, Reflect

1 Thessalonians 1:2-7

"Parents have a grave responsibility to give good example to their children. By knowing how to acknowledge their own failings to their children, parents will be better able to guide and correct them."
-The Catechism of the Catholic Church #2223

fifth, Examination

Lord, open my eyes and ears to be more honest with myself. Show me what has been happening to me and in me this day. Today, how have I experienced your love?

_____
_____
_____
_____
_____
_____
_____
_____
_____
_____

sixth Contrition

Today, what choices have been inadequate responses to your love?

_____
_____
_____
_____
_____
_____
_____

seventh, Hope

Lord, let me look with longing toward the future. How will I let you lead me to a brighter tomorrow?

_____
_____
_____
_____
_____
_____
_____

Weekly
Prayer

Prayer for Our Children from Ephesians 1:16–19

I pray that the God of our Lord Jesus Christ, the Father of glory, may give you a spirit of wisdom and of revelation in the knowledge of Him, having the eyes of your hearts enlightened, that you may know what is the hope to which He has called you, what are the riches of His glorious inheritance in the saints, and what is the immeasurable greatness of His power in us who believe.

Amen.

Prayer Goals

Prayer Intentions

For whom or what do I want to pray this week? Anyone who frustrates me, or has caused harm to myself or those I love. Anyone/anything who has touched my heart.

_____
_____
_____
_____
_____
_____
_____
_____

> "Not all of us can do great things. But we can do
> *small things with great love.*"
> —Mother Teresa of Calcutta

My "small things" this week:

_____
_____

Checklist

We draw a box next to any goals we want to make for ourselves this week, and check them off as we go.

_____
_____
_____
_____
_____
_____
_____
_____
_____
_____

Morning Offering

Evening Prayer or Liturgy of the Hours

Daily/Weekly Rosary

Angelus

Scripture Reading

Divine Mercy Chaplet

Other: _____

Weekday/Daily Mass

Confession

Fasting

Read a Saint Biography

Give alms or a donation

Novena

Volunteer at Homeless Shelter or Food Bank
(or other Corporal Work of Mercy)

first, Breathe

Breathe in ...
7 seconds.
Hold your breath ...
7 seconds.
Breathe out ...
7 seconds.

Repeat.

As many times
as you like.

second, Become aware of God's Presence

third, Thanksgiving

Lord, I realize that all, even myself, is a gift from you. Today, for what things am I most grateful?

fourth, Reflect

Psalm 16:9-11

"Pray, hope, and don't worry. Worry is useless.
God is merciful and will hear your prayer."
— St. Pio of Pietrelcina

fifth, Examination

Lord, open my eyes and ears to be more honest with myself. Show me what has been happening to me and in me this day. Today, how have I experienced your love?

_____
_____
_____
_____
_____
_____
_____
_____
_____
_____
_____
_____
_____
_____

sixth Contrition

Today, what choices have been inadequate responses to your love?

_____
_____
_____
_____
_____
_____
_____

seventh, Hope

Lord, let me look with longing toward the future. How will I let you lead me to a brighter tomorrow?

_____
_____
_____
_____
_____
_____
_____

Weekly
Prayer

Traditional Act of Contrition

Oh my God,
I am heartily sorry for having offended Thee,
And I detest all my sins, because I dread the loss of
heaven and the pains of hell;
But most of all because they offend Thee, my God,
Who art all-good and deserving of all my love.
I firmly resolve, with the help of Thy grace, to sin no
more and to avoid the near occasion of sin.
Amen.

Prayer Goals

Prayer Intentions

For whom or what do I want to pray this week? Anyone who frustrates me, or has caused harm to myself or those I love. Anyone/anything who has touched my heart.

_____
_____
_____
_____
_____
_____
_____
_____
_____

"Not all of us can do great things. But we can do *small things with great love.*"

-Mother Teresa of Calcutta

My "small things" this week:

_____
_____
_____
_____
_____
_____
_____
_____
_____
_____

Checklist

We draw a box next to any goals we want to make for ourselves this week, and check them off as we go.

Morning Offering

Evening Prayer or Liturgy of the Hours

Daily/Weekly Rosary

Angelus

Scripture Reading

Divine Mercy Chaplet

Other: _____

Weekday/Daily Mass

Confession

Fasting

Read a Saint Biography

Give alms or a donation

Novena

Volunteer at Homeless Shelter or Food Bank
(or other Corporal Work of Mercy)

first, Breathe

Breathe in ...
7 seconds.
Hold your breath ...
7 seconds.
Breathe out ...
7 seconds.

Repeat.

As many times
as you like.

second, Become aware of God's Presence

third, Thanksgiving

Lord, I realize that all, even myself, is a gift from you. Today, for what things am I most grateful?

fourth,
Reflect

Deuteronomy 31:7

"The secret to happiness is to live moment by moment and to thank God for what He is sending us every day in His goodness."
– St. Gianna Beretta Molla

fifth,
Examination

Lord, open my eyes and ears to be more honest with myself. Show me what has been happening to me and in me this day. Today, how have I experienced your love?

_____
_____
_____
_____
_____
_____
_____
_____
_____
_____
_____

sixth
Contrition

Today, what choices have been inadequate responses to your love?

_____
_____
_____
_____
_____
_____

seventh,
Hope

Lord, let me look with longing toward the future. How will I let you lead me to a brighter tomorrow?

_____
_____
_____
_____
_____
_____

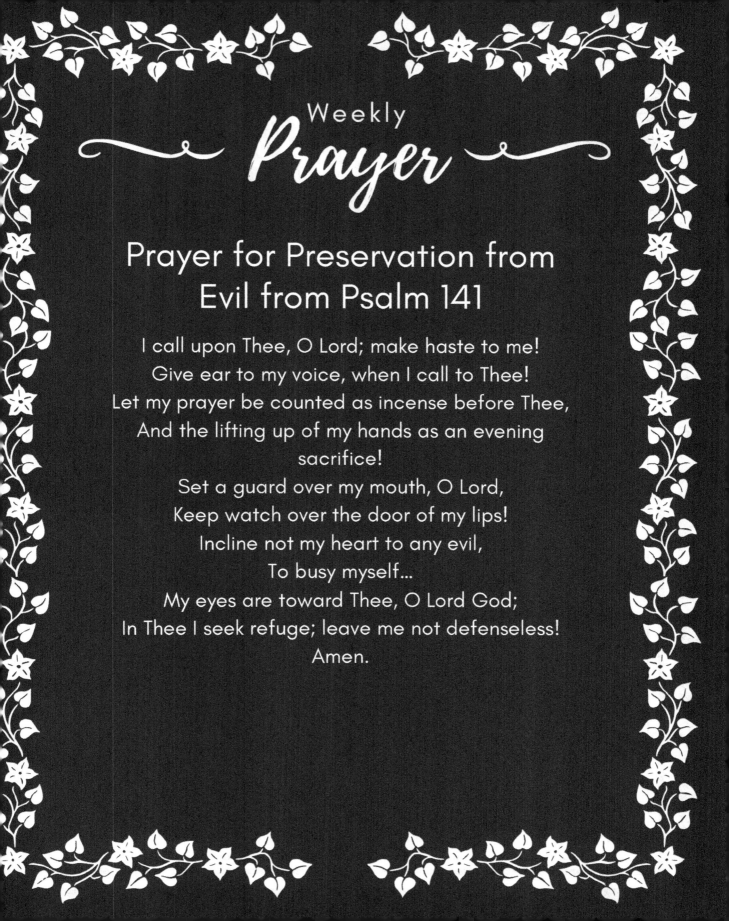

Weekly Prayer

Prayer for Preservation from Evil from Psalm 141

I call upon Thee, O Lord; make haste to me!
Give ear to my voice, when I call to Thee!
Let my prayer be counted as incense before Thee,
And the lifting up of my hands as an evening
sacrifice!
Set a guard over my mouth, O Lord,
Keep watch over the door of my lips!
Incline not my heart to any evil,
To busy myself...
My eyes are toward Thee, O Lord God;
In Thee I seek refuge; leave me not defenseless!
Amen.

Prayer Goals

Prayer Intentions

For whom or what do I want to pray this week? Anyone who frustrates me, or has caused harm to myself or those I love. Anyone/anything who has touched my heart.

_____
_____
_____
_____
_____
_____
_____

"Not all of us can do great things. But we can do *small things with great love.*"
-Mother Teresa of Calcutta

My "small things" this week:

_____
_____
_____
_____
_____
_____
_____
_____
_____
_____
_____
_____
_____

Checklist

We draw a box next to any goals we want to make for ourselves this week, and check them off as we go.

Morning Offering

Evening Prayer or Liturgy of the Hours

Daily/Weekly Rosary

Angelus

Scripture Reading

Divine Mercy Chaplet

Other: _____

Weekday/Daily Mass

Confession

Fasting

Read a Saint Biography

Give alms or a donation

Novena

Volunteer at Homeless Shelter or Food Bank
(or other Corporal Work of Mercy)

first, Breathe

Breathe in ...
7 seconds.
Hold your breath ...
7 seconds.
Breathe out ...
7 seconds.

Repeat.

As many times
as you like.

second, Become aware of God's Presence

third, Thanksgiving

Lord, I realize that all, even myself, is a gift from you. Today, for what things am I most grateful?

fourth, Reflect

Matthew 6:33

"You will never be happy if your happiness depends on getting solely what you want. Change the focus. Get a new center. Will what God wills, and your joy no man shall take from you."
– Venerable Fulton Sheen

fifth, Examination

Lord, open my eyes and ears to be more honest with myself. Show me what has been happening to me and in me this day. Today, how have I experienced your love?

sixth, Contrition

Today, what choices have been inadequate responses to your love?

seventh, Hope

Lord, let me look with longing toward the future. How will I let you lead me to a brighter tomorrow?

Weekly
Prayer

Magnificat

My soul proclaims the greatness of the Lord,
My spirit rejoices in God my Savior;
For he has looked with favor on His lowly servant.
From this day all generations will call me blessed:
The Almighty has done great things for me,
And holy is His Name.
He has mercy on those who fear Him
in every generation.
He has shown the strength of His arm,
He has scattered the proud in their conceit.
He has cast down the mighty from their thrones,
And has lifted up the lowly.
He has filled the hungry with good things,
And the rich he has sent away empty.
He has come to the help of His servant Israel
For he has remembered His promise of mercy,
The promise He made to our fathers,
To Abraham and His children forever.
Amen.

Prayer Goals

Prayer Intentions

For whom or what do I want to pray this week? Anyone who frustrates me, or has caused harm to myself or those I love. Anyone/anything who has touched my heart.

_____
_____
_____
_____
_____
_____
_____
_____

"Not all of us can do great things. But we can do _small things with great love._"

-Mother Teresa of Calcutta

My "small things" this week:

_____
_____
_____
_____
_____
_____
_____
_____
_____
_____

Checklist

We draw a box next to any goals we want to make for ourselves this week, and check them off as we go.

Morning Offering

Evening Prayer or Liturgy of the Hours

Daily/Weekly Rosary

Angelus

Scripture Reading

Divine Mercy Chaplet

Other: _____

Weekday/Daily Mass

Confession

Fasting

Read a Saint Biography

Give alms or a donation

Novena

Volunteer at Homeless Shelter or Food Bank
(or other Corporal Work of Mercy)

first, Breathe

Breathe in ...
7 seconds.
Hold your breath ...
7 seconds.
Breathe out ...
7 seconds.

Repeat.

As many times
as you like.

second, Become aware of God's Presence

third, Thanksgiving

Lord, I realize that all, even myself, is a gift from you. Today, for what things am I most grateful?

fourth,
Reflect

John 14:1-2

"Worrying does not empty tomorrow of its troubles. It empties today of its strength."
– Corrie Ten Boom (Concentration Camp Survivor, Christian Writer/Speaker)

fifth,
Examination

Lord, open my eyes and ears to be more honest with myself. Show me what has been happening to me and in me this day. Today, how have I experienced your love?

_____
_____
_____
_____
_____
_____
_____
_____
_____
_____

sixth
Contrition

Today, what choices have been inadequate responses to your love?

_____
_____
_____
_____
_____
_____

seventh,
Hope

Lord, let me look with longing toward the future. How will I let you lead me to a brighter tomorrow?

_____
_____
_____
_____
_____
_____

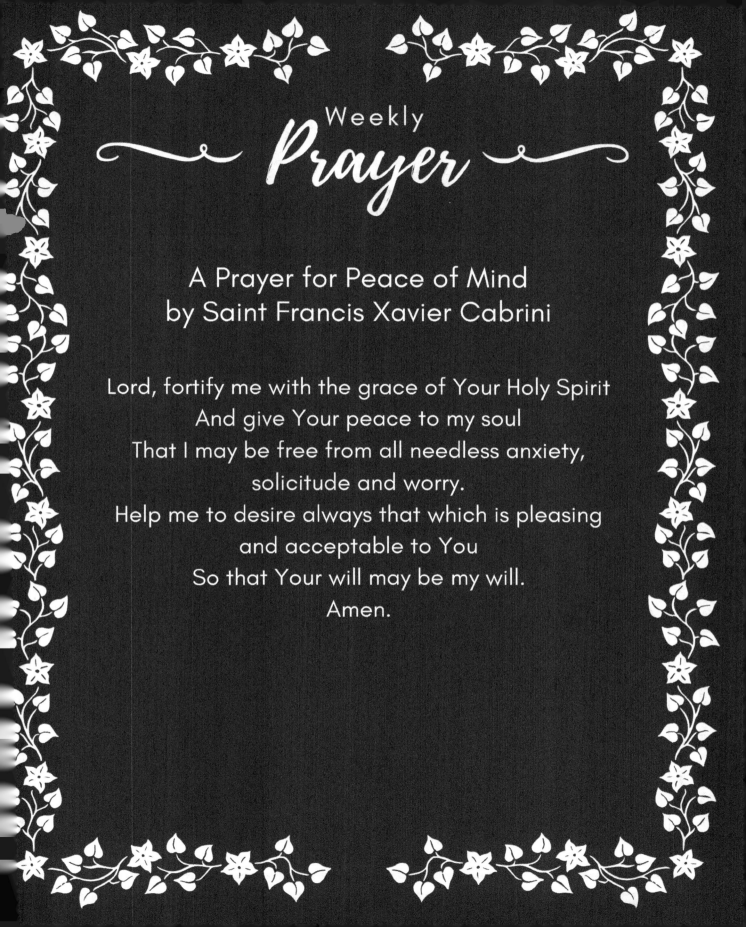

Weekly
Prayer

A Prayer for Peace of Mind
by Saint Francis Xavier Cabrini

Lord, fortify me with the grace of Your Holy Spirit
And give Your peace to my soul
That I may be free from all needless anxiety,
solicitude and worry.
Help me to desire always that which is pleasing
and acceptable to You
So that Your will may be my will.
Amen.

Prayer Goals

Prayer Intentions

For whom or what do I want to pray this week? Anyone who frustrates me, or has caused harm to myself or those I love. Anyone/anything who has touched my heart.

_____
_____
_____
_____
_____
_____
_____

> "Not all of us can do great things. But we can do *small things with great love.*"
> —Mother Teresa of Calcutta

My "small things" this week:

_____
_____
_____
_____
_____
_____
_____
_____
_____
_____
_____
_____
_____
_____

Checklist

We draw a box next to any goals we want to make for ourselves this week, and check them off as we go.

Morning Offering

Evening Prayer or Liturgy of the Hours

Daily/Weekly Rosary

Angelus

Scripture Reading

Divine Mercy Chaplet

Other: _____

Weekday/Daily Mass

Confession

Fasting

Read a Saint Biography

Give alms or a donation

Novena

Volunteer at Homeless Shelter or Food Bank
(or other Corporal Work of Mercy)

first, Breathe

Breathe in ...
7 seconds.
Hold your breath ...
7 seconds.
Breathe out ...
7 seconds.

Repeat.

As many times
as you like.

second, Become aware of God's Presence

third, Thanksgiving

Lord, I realize that all, even myself, is a gift from you. Today, for what things am I most grateful?

fourth,
Reflect

Colossians 3:12–13

"Yesterday is gone. Tomorrow has not yet come.
We only have today. Let us begin."
– St. Teresa of Calcutta

fifth,
Examination

Lord, open my eyes and ears to be more honest with myself. Show me what has been happening to me and in me this day. Today, how have I experienced your love?

_____
_____
_____
_____
_____
_____
_____
_____
_____
_____
_____
_____

sixth
Contrition

Today, what choices have been inadequate responses to your love?

_____
_____
_____
_____
_____
_____

seventh,
Hope

Lord, let me look with longing toward the future. How will I let you lead me to a brighter tomorrow?

_____
_____
_____
_____
_____
_____

Weekly
Prayer

Psalm 23

The Lord is my shepherd, I shall not want;
He makes me lie down in green pastures.
He leads me beside still waters;
He restores my soul.
He leads me in paths of righteousness
For His name's sake.

Even though I walk through the valley
of the shadow of death,
I fear no evil;
For thou art with me;
Thy rod and Thy staff,
They comfort me.

Thou preparest a table before me
In the presence of my enemies;
Thou anointest my head with oil,
My cup overflows.
Surely goodness and mercy shall follow me
All the days of my life;
And I shall dwell in the house of the Lord forever.
Amen.

Prayer Goals

Prayer Intentions

For whom or what do I want to pray this week? Anyone who frustrates me, or has caused harm to myself or those I love. Anyone/anything who has touched my heart.

_____
_____
_____
_____
_____
_____
_____
_____

"Not all of us can do great things. But we can do *small things with great love.*"

-Mother Teresa of Calcutta

My "small things" this week:

_____
_____
_____
_____
_____
_____
_____
_____
_____
_____
_____
_____
_____
_____

Checklist

We draw a box next to any goals we want to make for ourselves this week, and check them off as we go.

Morning Offering

Evening Prayer or Liturgy of the Hours

Daily/Weekly Rosary

Angelus

Scripture Reading

Divine Mercy Chaplet

Other: _____

Weekday/Daily Mass

Confession

Fasting

Read a Saint Biography

Give alms or a donation

Novena

Volunteer at Homeless Shelter or Food Bank
(or other Corporal Work of Mercy)

first, Breathe

Breathe in ...
7 seconds.
Hold your breath ...
7 seconds.
Breathe out ...
7 seconds.

Repeat.

As many times
as you like.

second, Become aware of God's Presence

third, Thanksgiving

Lord, I realize that all, even myself, is a gift from you. Today, for what things am I most grateful?

fourth, Reflect

John 14:26

"Seen from the outside, all these trials are frightening. We wondered if we could ever confront anything similar. But each step is accompanied by a necessary grace."
– Chiara Corbella Petrillo, Servant of God

fifth, Examination

Lord, open my eyes and ears to be more honest with myself. Show me what has been happening to me and in me this day. Today, how have I experienced your love?

_____
_____
_____
_____
_____
_____
_____
_____
_____
_____

sixth, Contrition

Today, what choices have been inadequate responses to your love?

_____
_____
_____
_____
_____
_____

seventh, Hope

Lord, let me look with longing toward the future. How will I let you lead me to a brighter tomorrow?

_____
_____
_____
_____
_____
_____

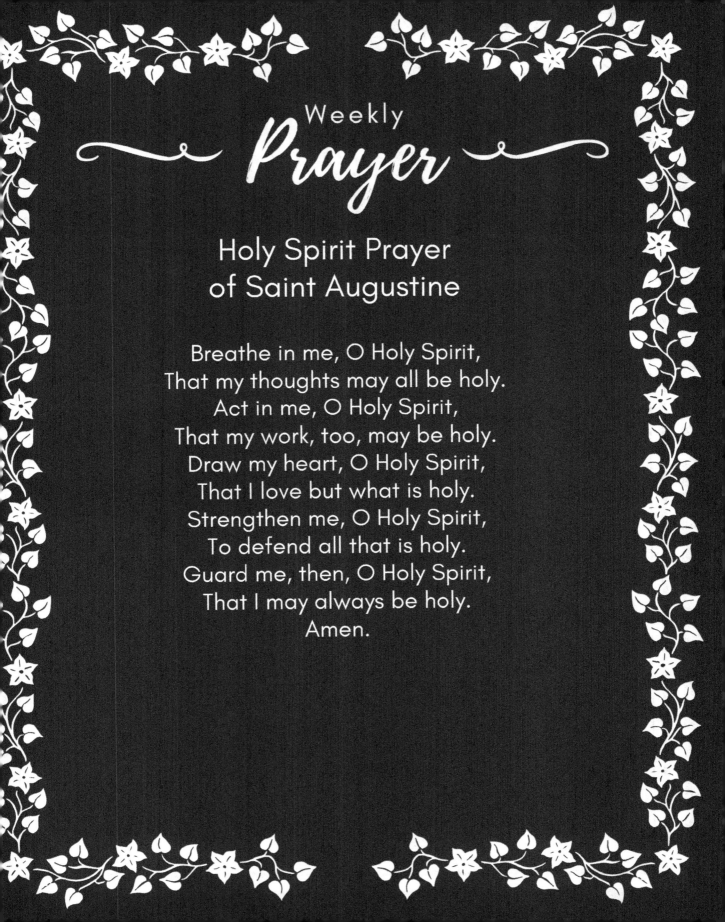

Weekly
Prayer

Holy Spirit Prayer
of Saint Augustine

Breathe in me, O Holy Spirit,
That my thoughts may all be holy.
Act in me, O Holy Spirit,
That my work, too, may be holy.
Draw my heart, O Holy Spirit,
That I love but what is holy.
Strengthen me, O Holy Spirit,
To defend all that is holy.
Guard me, then, O Holy Spirit,
That I may always be holy.
Amen.

Prayer Goals

Prayer Intentions

For whom or what do I want to pray this week? Anyone who frustrates me, or has caused harm to myself or those I love. Anyone/anything who has touched my heart.

_____
_____
_____
_____
_____
_____
_____
_____

> "Not all of us can do great things. But we can do
>
> *small things with great love.*"
>
> -Mother Teresa of Calcutta

My "small things" this week:

_____
_____
_____
_____
_____
_____
_____
_____
_____
_____
_____

Checklist

We draw a box next to any goals we want to make for ourselves this week, and check them off as we go.

Morning Offering

Evening Prayer or Liturgy of the Hours

Daily/Weekly Rosary

Angelus

Scripture Reading

Divine Mercy Chaplet

Other: _____

Weekday/Daily Mass

Confession Fasting

Read a Saint Biography

Give alms or a donation

Novena

Volunteer at Homeless Shelter or Food Bank
(or other Corporal Work of Mercy)

first, Breathe

Breathe in …
7 seconds.
Hold your breath …
7 seconds.
Breathe out …
7 seconds.

Repeat.

As many times
as you like.

second, Become aware of God's Presence

third, Thanksgiving

Lord, I realize that all, even myself, is a gift from you. Today, for what things am I most grateful?

fourth, Reflect

Deuteronomy 30:19

"We forget that life doesn't have to be perfect to be wonderful. And that each day is a delicate dance between making things happen and letting them happen."
-Anonymous

fifth, Examination

Lord, open my eyes and ears to be more honest with myself. Show me what has been happening to me and in me this day. Today, how have I experienced your love?

_____
_____
_____
_____
_____
_____
_____
_____
_____
_____

sixth, Contrition

Today, what choices have been inadequate responses to your love?

_____
_____
_____
_____
_____
_____

seventh, Hope

Lord, let me look with longing toward the future. How will I let you lead me to a brighter tomorrow?

_____
_____
_____
_____
_____
_____

Weekly *Prayer*

Morning Prayer
of St. Therese of Lisieux

O my God! I offer Thee all my actions of this day for the intentions and for the glory of the Sacred Heart of Jesus. I desire to sanctify every beat of my heart, my every thought, my simplest works, by uniting them to Your infinite merits; and I wish to make reparation for my sins by casting them into the furnace of Your Merciful Love. O my God! I ask of Thee for myself and for those whom I hold dear, the grace to fulfill perfectly Thy Holy Will, to accept for love of Thee the joys and sorrows of this passing life, so that we may one day be united together in heaven for all eternity. Amen.

Prayer Goals

Prayer Intentions

For whom or what do I want to pray this week? Anyone who frustrates me, or has caused harm to myself or those I love. Anyone/anything who has touched my heart.

_____
_____
_____
_____
_____
_____
_____
_____
_____
_____

"Not all of us can do great things. But we can do

small things with great love.

-Mother Teresa of Calcutta

My "small things" this week:

_____
_____
_____
_____
_____
_____
_____
_____
_____
_____
_____
_____

Checklist

We draw a box next to any goals we want to make for ourselves this week, and check them off as we go.

Morning Offering

Evening Prayer or Liturgy of the Hours

Daily/Weekly Rosary

Angelus

Scripture Reading

Divine Mercy Chaplet

Other: _____

Weekday/Daily Mass

Confession

Fasting

Read a Saint Biography

Give alms or a donation

Novena

Volunteer at Homeless Shelter or Food Bank
(or other Corporal Work of Mercy)

Week Fifty

first, *Breathe*

Breathe in ...
7 seconds.
Hold your breath ...
7 seconds.
Breathe out ...
7 seconds.

Repeat.

As many times
as you like.

second, Become aware of *God's Presence*

third, *Thanksgiving*

Lord, I realize that all, even myself, is a gift from you. Today, for what things am I most grateful?

fourth, Reflect

Exodus 14:14

"Not an hour passes without the enormity of the task I've taken on bringing me to my knees. This work of... raising hearts and souls and bodies is hard. It is more than I can do in my own strength. Even so, more than anything else, I desire to... mother in a way that pleases God."
– Sarah Mackenzie

fifth, Examination

Lord, open my eyes and ears to be more honest with myself. Show me what has been happening to me and in me this day. Today, how have I experienced your love?

_____
_____
_____
_____
_____
_____
_____
_____
_____
_____
_____
_____

sixth Contrition

Today, what choices have been inadequate responses to your love?

_____
_____
_____
_____
_____
_____
_____
_____

seventh, Hope

Lord, let me look with longing toward the future. How will I let you lead me to a brighter tomorrow?

_____
_____
_____
_____
_____
_____
_____
_____

Weekly
Prayer

Prayer for Support
by Saint John Henry Newman

O Lord, support us all the day long, until the shadows lengthen, and the evening comes, and the busy world is hushed, and the fever of life is over, and our work is done. Then in your mercy, grant us a safe lodging and a holy rest, and peace at the last. Through Jesus Christ Our Lord, Amen.

Prayer Goals

Prayer Intentions

For whom or what do I want to pray this week? Anyone who frustrates me, or has caused harm to myself or those I love. Anyone/anything who has touched my heart.

_____
_____
_____
_____
_____
_____
_____

> "Not all of us can do great things. But we can do
> *small things with great love.*"
> -Mother Teresa of Calcutta

My "small things" this week:

_____

Checklist

We draw a box next to any goals we want to make for ourselves this week, and check them off as we go.

_____
_____
_____
_____
_____
_____
_____
_____

Morning Offering

Evening Prayer or Liturgy of the Hours

Daily/Weekly Rosary

Angelus

Scripture Reading

Divine Mercy Chaplet

Other: _____

Weekday/Daily Mass

Confession

Fasting

Read a Saint Biography

Give alms or a donation

Novena

Volunteer at Homeless Shelter or Food Bank
(or other Corporal Work of Mercy)

first, Breathe

*

Breathe in ...
7 seconds.
Hold your breath ...
7 seconds.
Breathe out ...
7 seconds.

Repeat.

As many times
as you like.

second,
Become aware of God's Presence

third, Thanksgiving

Lord, I realize that all, even myself, is a gift from you. Today, for what things am I most grateful?

1 Corinthians 13:2

"The home is well suited for education in the virtues. This requires an apprenticeship in self-denial, sound judgment, and self-mastery – the preconditions of all true freedom. Parents should teach their children to subordinate the 'material and instinctual dimensions to interior and spiritual ones.'"
-The Catechism of the Catholic Church #2223

fifth,
Examination

Lord, open my eyes and ears to be more honest with myself. Show me what has been happening to me and in me this day. Today, how have I experienced your love?

_____
_____
_____
_____
_____
_____
_____

sixth
Contrition

Today, what choices have been inadequate responses to your love?

_____
_____
_____
_____

seventh,
Hope

Lord, let me look with longing toward the future. How will I let you lead me to a brighter tomorrow?

_____
_____
_____
_____

Weekly
Prayer

Prayer of
St. Thomas Aquinas

Grant me grace, O merciful God,
To desire ardently all that is pleasing to You,
To examine it prudently,
To acknowledge it truthfully,
And to accomplish it perfectly,
For the praise and glory of Your name.
Amen.

Prayer Goals

Prayer Intentions

For whom or what do I want to pray this week? Anyone who frustrates me, or has caused harm to myself or those I love. Anyone/anything who has touched my heart.

_____
_____
_____
_____
_____
_____
_____
_____

"Not all of us can do great things. But we can do

small things with great love."
-Mother Teresa of Calcutta

My "small things" this week:

_____
_____
_____
_____
_____
_____
_____
_____
_____
_____
_____
_____

Checklist

We draw a box next to any goals we want to make for ourselves this week, and check them off as we go.

Morning Offering

Evening Prayer or Liturgy of the Hours

Daily/Weekly Rosary

Angelus

Scripture Reading

Divine Mercy Chaplet

Other: _____

Weekday/Daily Mass

Confession

Fasting

Read a Saint Biography

Give alms or a donation

Novena

Volunteer at Homeless Shelter or Food Bank
(or other Corporal Work of Mercy)

first, Breathe

Week Fifty-Two

Breathe in ...
7 seconds.
Hold your breath ...
7 seconds.
Breathe out ...
7 seconds.

Repeat.

As many times
as you like.

second,
Become aware of
God's Presence

third,
Thanksgiving

Lord, I realize that all, even myself, is a gift from you. Today, for what things am I most grateful?

fourth, Reflect

Deuteronomy 32:2

"[Parental] authority must be tempered...with loving kindness and patient encouragement. To temper authority with kindness is to triumph in the struggle which belongs to your duty as parents...All those who would advantageously rule over others, must as an essential element, first dominate themselves, their passions, their impressions..." – Pope Pius XII

fifth, Examination

Lord, open my eyes and ears to be more honest with myself. Show me what has been happening to me and in me this day. Today, how have I experienced your love?

_____
_____
_____
_____
_____
_____
_____
_____
_____
_____

sixth, Contrition

Today, what choices have been inadequate responses to your love?

_____
_____
_____
_____
_____
_____

seventh, Hope

Lord, let me look with longing toward the future. How will I let you lead me to a brighter tomorrow?

_____
_____
_____
_____
_____
_____

Weekly Prayer

The Benedictus

Blessed be the Lord, the God of Israel;
He has come to His people and set them free.
He has raised up for us a mighty savior,
born of the house of His servant David.

Through His holy prophets He promised of old
that He would save us from our enemies,
from the hands of all who hate us.
He promised to show mercy to our fathers
and to remember His holy covenant.

This was the oath He swore to our father Abraham:
to set us free from the hands of our enemies,
free to worship Him without fear,
holy and righteous in His sight all the days of our life.

You, my child, shall be called the prophet of the Most High;
for you will go before the Lord to prepare His way,
to give His people knowledge of salvation
by the forgiveness of their sins.

In the tender compassion of our God
the dawn from on high shall break upon us,
to shine on those who dwell in darkness and the shadow of death,
and to guide our feet into the way of peace.
Amen.

Prayer Goals

Prayer Intentions

For whom or what do I want to pray this week? Anyone who frustrates me, or has caused harm to myself or those I love. Anyone/anything who has touched my heart.

_____
_____
_____
_____
_____
_____
_____
_____
_____

"Not all of us can do great things. But we can do

small things with great love."

-Mother Teresa of Calcutta

My "small things" this week:

_____
_____

Checklist

We draw a box next to any goals we want to make for ourselves this week, and check them off as we go.

_____
_____
_____
_____
_____
_____
_____
_____
_____
_____
_____
_____

Morning Offering

Evening Prayer or Liturgy of the Hours

Daily/Weekly Rosary

Angelus

Scripture Reading

Divine Mercy Chaplet

Other: _____

Weekday/Daily Mass

Confession

Fasting

Read a Saint Biography

Give alms or a donation

Novena

Volunteer at Homeless Shelter or Food Bank
(or other Corporal Work of Mercy)

About the Author:
Mary Nadeau Reed

M ary Nadeau Reed was born and raised just outside New Orleans, Louisiana. She graduated from Tulane University with a degree in English and Psychology, and completed her Masters in Theology at Notre Dame Seminary. She is now homeschooling her four children, having been homeschooled through high school herself. Mary, her husband Cody, and their children, RoseMary, Francis, Thérèse, and Elizabeth now live in the Sans Souci Forest (north of New Orleans). *Sans souci* means "without worry", so Mary invites us all, in the words of St. Pio, to "pray, hope, and *don't worry.*"

About the Publisher

SCOTT L. SMITH, JR., *J.D., M.T.S.*

Scott L. Smith, Jr. is a Catholic author, attorney, theologian, publisher, and 13th generation Pointe Coupeean. He and his wife Ashton are the parents of six wild-eyed children and live in their hometown of New Roads, Louisiana.

Smith is currently serving as the Grand Knight of his local Knights of Columbus council, co-host of the Catholic Nerds Podcast, and the board of the Men of the Immaculata. Smith has served as a minister and teacher far and wide: from Angola, Louisiana's maximum-security prison, to the slums of Kibera, Kenya.

Smith's books include *Consecration to St. Joseph for Children & Families*, which he co-authored with Fr. Donald Calloway, *Pray the Rosary with St. Pope John Paul II*, *The Catholic ManBook*, *Lord of the Rings & the Eucharist*, among other titles. His fiction includes *The Seventh Word* and the *Cajun Zombie Chronicles*, horror novels set in New Roads, Louisiana.

Scott regularly contributes to his blog, "The Scott Smith Blog" at www.thescottsmithblog.com, winner of the Fisher's Net Award for Best Catholic Blog. Scott's other books can be found at the Holy Water Books website, holywaterbooks.com, as well as on Amazon.

More Catholic Prayer Journals from Holy Water Books

Holy Water Books has published a series of prayer journals, including *The Pray, Hope, & Don't Worry* Prayer Journal to Overcome Stress and Anxiety.

Pray, Hope, & Don't Worry: Catholic Prayer Journal for Women

Daily Bible verses and quotes from the Saints to reflect on. Use the prayer journal either as a 52-day or 52-week retreat to overcome stress and worry.

There is also a separate edition for women of other Christian faiths:
Pray, Hope, & Don't Worry Women's Prayer Journal For Overcoming Anxiety: A 52-week Guided Devotional of Prayers & Bible Verses to Conquer Stress & Fear.

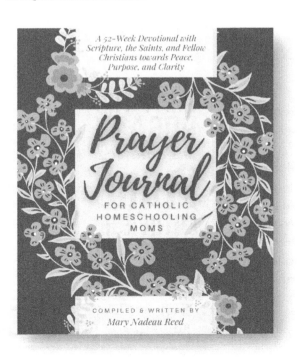

Prayer Journal for Catholic Homeschooling Moms: A 52-week Guided Devotional with Scripture, the Saints, and fellow Christians towards Peace, Purpose, and Clarity

Using a similar 52-day or 52-week format as the *Pray, Hope, and Don't Worry* Prayer Journal above, this journal was created by Mary Nadeau Reed specifically for Catholic homeschooling moms.

Rosary Devotionals from Holy Water Books:
Pray the Rosary with St. John Paul II

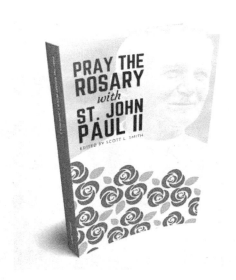

St. John Paul II said "the Rosary is my favorite prayer." So what could possibly make praying the Rosary even better? Praying the Rosary with St. John Paul II!

This book includes a reflection from John Paul II for every mystery of the Rosary. You will find John Paul II's biblical reflections on the twenty mysteries of the Rosary that provide practical insights to help you not only understand the twenty mysteries but also live them.

St. John Paul II said "The Rosary is my favorite prayer. A marvelous prayer! Marvelous in its simplicity and its depth. In the prayer we repeat many times the words that the Virgin Mary heard from the Archangel, and from her kinswoman Elizabeth."

St. John Paul II said "the Rosary is the storehouse of countless blessings." In this new book, he will help you dig even deeper into the treasures contained within the Rosary.

You will also learn St. John Paul II's spirituality of the Rosary: "To pray the Rosary is to hand over our burdens to the merciful hearts of Christ and His mother." "The Rosary, though clearly Marian in character, is at heart a Christ-centered prayer. It has all the depth of the gospel message in its entirety. It is an echo of the prayer of Mary, her perennial Magnificat for the work of the redemptive Incarnation which began in her virginal womb." **Take the Rosary to a whole new level with St. John Paul the Great! St. John Paul II, *pray for us!***

Pray the Rosary with Blessed Anne Catherine Emmerich

Pray the Rosary like never before! Enter into the mysteries of the Rosary through the eyes of the famous 19th-century Catholic mystic: Blessed Anne Catherine Emmerich.

Incredibly, God gave this nun the special privilege of beholding innumerable Biblical events from Creation to Christ's Passion and beyond. You may have already seen many of her visions, as depicted in the 2004 film The Passion of the Christ.

Never before have Emmerich's revelations been collected in a single volume to help you pray the Rosary. Emmerich was able to describe the events of the Rosary in intimate, exquisite detail. Adding depth and texture to the Gospel accounts, these passages will greatly enhance your experience of the meditations of the Rosary. Enjoy!

CLASSIC CATHOLIC REPRINTS & NEW TRANSLATIONS

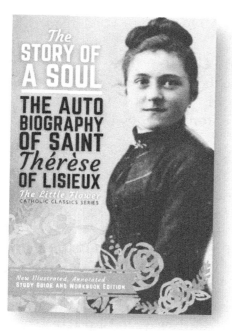

THE STORY OF A SOUL, THE AUTOBIOGRAPHY OF SAINT THERESE OF LISIEUX: NEW ILLUSTRATED, ANNOTATED STUDY GUIDE AND WORKBOOK EDITION

One of the most popular biographies, not just saint biographies, of ALL TIME. Saint Thérèse, one of the most beautiful souls of modern times, also gave us the most beautiful spiritualities of modern times: the "Little Way" of the "little flower" of Jesus.

Read this with your Catholic book group. This edition features additional sections with study questions to help your group dig into the spiritual wisdom of the Little Flower.

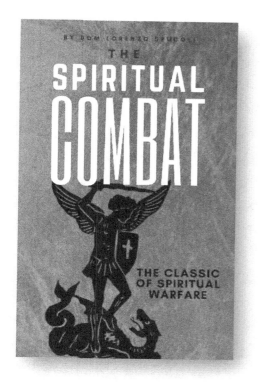

THE SPIRITUAL COMBAT: THE CLASSIC MANUAL ON SPIRITUAL WARFARE, BY DOM LORENZO SCUPOLI

St. Francis de Sales always carried this book in his pocket! The Spiritual Combat is the classic manual of spiritual warfare. Its wisdom has helped form the souls of the Church's greatest saints. Now this book can do the same thing for you. It's no longer fashionable to speak about the realities of the devil and demons, and so the world has become more vulnerable than ever before. The Christian life is a battle between God and the forces of darkness.

This is the *Art of War* for the Christian. Pick up your sword and fight! Here, Father Lorenzo Scupoli helps guide you through this spiritual battle, so that you can win - decisively - the war for your soul. Pick up the sword of prayer and conquer the evil which afflicts you, and through you, your family, your friends, and the world. Don't go into battle alone. Go with Christ and this classic combat manual.

THE SEVEN LAST WORDS SPOKEN FROM THE CROSS BY ST. ROBERT BELLARMINE S.J.

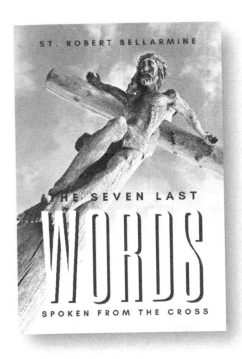

Come, sit at the foot of the Cross!

These seven words were the "last sermon" of the Savior of the World. Jesus' words from the Cross contain everything that the prophets foretold about His preaching, suffering, and miracles.

The Seven Last Words Spoken from the Cross is a powerful reflection on the final words of Jesus Christ. The author, St. Robert Bellarmine, was a major figure in the Catholic Counter-Reformation and his insights are as profound now as ever, perhaps more than ever.

Deepen the Way of the Cross! Use Bellarmine's contemplations of Christ's words to enrich your Lenten journey to Good Friday and Easter. The Seven Last Words Spoken from the Cross is a wealth of insights for the whole of the Christian life, which points always to Christ, who was lifted up on the Cross so "that everyone who believes in Him may have eternal life."

ST. LOUIS DE MONTFORT'S TOTAL CONSECRATION TO JESUS THROUGH MARY: NEW, DAY-BY-DAY, EASIER-TO-READ TRANSLATION

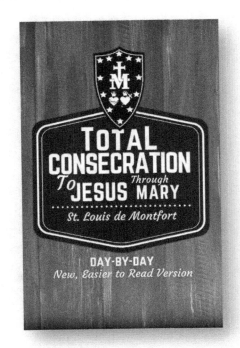

Featured on HALLOW, the #1 Catholic Prayer App and narrated by Sister Miriam Heidland!

Popes and Saints have called this single greatest book of Marian spirituality ever written. In a newly translated day-by-day format, follow St. Louis de Montfort's classic work on the spiritual way to Jesus Christ though the Blessed Virgin Mary.

Beloved by countless souls, this book sums up, not just the majesty of the Blessed Mother, but the entire Christian life. St. Louis de Montfort calls this the "short, easy, secure, and perfect" path to Christ. It is the way chosen by Jesus, Himself.

Prayer Like a Warrior: Spiritual Combat & War Room Prayer Guide

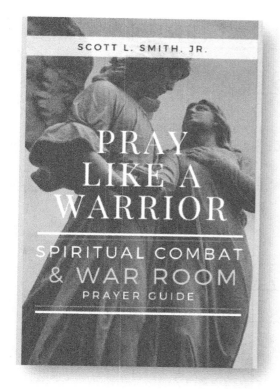

Don't get caught unarmed! Develop your Prayer Room Strategy and Battle Plan.

An invisible war rages around you. Something or someone is attacking you, unseen, unheard, yet felt throughout every aspect of your life. An army of demons under the banner of Satan has a singular focus: your destruction and that of everyone you know and love.

You need to protect your soul, your heart, your mind, your marriage, your children, your relationships, your resolve, your dreams, and your destiny.

Do you want to be a Prayer Warrior, but don't know where to start? The Devil's battle plan depends on catching you unarmed and unaware. If you're tired of being pushed around and wrecked by sin and distraction, this book is for you.

Do you feel uncomfortable speaking to God? Do you struggle with distractions in the presence of Almighty God? Praying to God may feel foreign, tedious, or like a ritual, and is He really listening? What if He never hears, never responds? This book will show you that God always listens and always answers.

In this book, you will learn how to prayer effectively no matter where you are mentally, what your needs are, or how you are feeling:

- Prayers when angry or your heart is troubled
- Prayers for fear, stress, and hopelessness
- Prayers to overcome pride, unforgiveness, and bitterness
- Prayers for rescue and shelter

Or are you looking to upgrade your prayer life? This book is for you, too. You already know that a prayer war room is a powerful weapon in spiritual warfare. Prepare for God to pour out blessings on your life.

Our broken world and broken souls need the prayers and direction found in this book. Don't waste time fumbling through your prayer life. Pray more strategically when you have a War Room Battle Plan. Jesus showed His disciples how to pray and He wants to show you how to pray, too.

MATERIALS FOR THE CATHOLIC NERD IN ALL OF US:

CATHOLIC NERDS PODCAST

As you might have noticed, Scott is well-credentialed as a nerd. Check out Scott's podcast: the Catholic Nerds Podcast on iTunes, Spotify, Google Play, and wherever good podcasts are found!

THE THEOLOGY OF SCI-FI: THE CHRISTIAN'S COMPANION TO THE GALAXY

NOW ALSO AN AUDIOBOOK! Fold space using the spice mélange and travel from "a long time ago in a galaxy far, far away" to the planet Krypton, from Trantor to Terminus, and back to the scorched skies of earth.

Did you know there is a Virgin Birth at the core of *Star Wars*? A Jewish Messiah of *Dune*? A Holy Family in *Superman*? A Jesus and Judas in *The Matrix*? And the Catholic Church is Asimov's *Foundation*?

This book covers a lot of territory. It spans galaxies and universes. Nevertheless, the great expanse of human imagination will forever be captivated by the events of the little town of Bethlehem.

There is a reason that all of mankind's stories overlap, coincide, correlate, and copy. Like it or not, all mankind bears the same indelible stamp, the mark of Christ. Why should there be a singular story binding us all? Unless we are truly all bound as one human family. At the core of the Monomyth is not another myth, a neat coincidence, but a reality—the reality of Jesus Christ.

At the heart of the Monomyth is a man, a very real man. The God-Man. The source and summit of all hero stories and myths ever told, both before and after those short 33 years in First Century Israel.

LORD OF THE RINGS & THE EUCHARIST

NOW AN AUDIOBOOK!

What is "the one great thing to love on earth", according to J. R. R. Tolkien, the author of The Lord of the Rings? The Eucharist! Tolkien made sure his one great love was woven throughout his books. It's easy to find if you know where to look. In Smith's new book, find Tolkien's hidden Eucharist!

The Lord of the Rings can't be fully understood without understanding its hidden Eucharistic significance. What's more, perhaps: J. R. R. Tolkien can't be fully understood apart from his Catholic identity and his devotion to the Eucharist.

Are you ready to read Lord of the Rings like you never have before?

WHAT YOU NEED TO KNOW ABOUT MARY BUT WERE NEVER TAUGHT

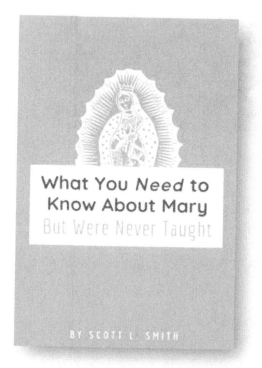

NOW AN AUDIOBOOK!

Give a robust defense of the Blessed Mother using Scripture. Now, more than ever, every Catholic needs to learn how to defend their mother, the Blessed Mother. Because now, more than ever, the family is under attack and needs its Mother.

Discover the love story, hidden within the whole of Scripture, of the Father for his daughter, the Holy Spirit for his spouse, and the Son for his MOTHER.

This collection of essays and the All Saints University course made to accompany it will demonstrate through Scripture how the Immaculate Conception of Mary was prophesied in Genesis.

It will also show how the Virgin Mary is the New Eve, the New Ark, and the New Queen of Israel.

AND FOR THE CATHOLIC MAN ...

THE CATHOLIC MANBOOK

Do you want to reach Catholic Man LEVEL: EXPERT? *The Catholic ManBook* is your handbook to achieving Sainthood, manly Sainthood. Find the following resources inside, plus many others:

- Top Catholic Apps, Websites, and Blogs
- Everything you need to pray the Rosary
- The Most Effective Daily Prayers & Novenas, including the Emergency Novena
- Going to Confession and Eucharistic Adoration like a boss!
- Mastering the Catholic Liturgical Calendar

The Catholic ManBook contains the collective wisdom of The Men of the Immaculata, of saints, priests and laymen, fathers and sons, single and married. Holiness is at your fingertips. Get your copy today.

This edition also includes a revised and updated St. Louis de Montfort Marian consecration. Follow the prayers in a day-by-day format.

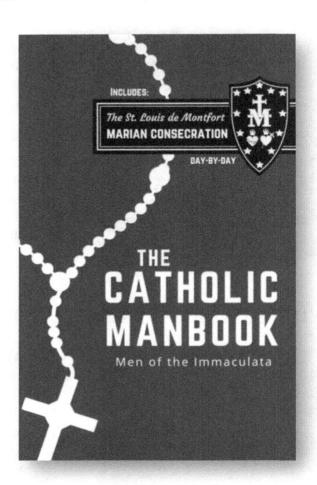

Blessed is He Who ...
Models of Catholic Manhood

BIOGRAPHIES OF CATHOLIC BLESSEDS

You are the average of the five people you spend the most time with, so spend more time with the Saints! Here are several men that you need to get to know whatever your age or station in life. These short biographies will give you an insight into how to live better, however you're living.

From Kings to computer nerds, old married couples to single teenagers, these men gave us extraordinary examples of holiness:

- Pier Giorgio Frassati & Carlo Acutis — Here are two extraordinary **young men**, an athlete and a computer nerd, living on either side of the 20th Century

- Two men of royal stock, Francesco II and Archduke Eu-gen, lived lives of holiness despite all the world conspiring against them.

- There's also the **simple husband and father**, Blessed Luigi. Though he wasn't a king, he can help all of us treat the women in our lives as queens.

Blessed Is He Who ... Models of Catholic Manhood explores the lives of six men who found their greatness in Christ and His Bride, the Church. In six succinct chapters, the authors, noted historian Brian J. Costello and theologian and attorney Scott L. Smith, share with you the uncommon lives of exceptional men who will one day be numbered among the Saints of Heaven, men who can bring all of us closer to sainthood.

Ever heard of Catholic HORROR Novels?

It's time to evangelize *all* readers …

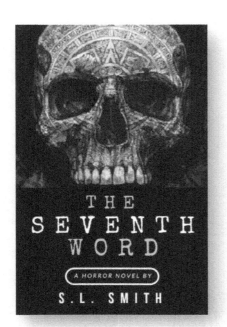

THE SEVENTH WORD

The FIRST Pro-Life Horror Novel!

Pro-Life hero, Abby Johnson, called it "legit scary … I don't like reading this as night! … It was good, it was so good … it was terrifying, but good."

The First Word came with Cain, who killed the first child of man. The Third Word was Pharaoh's instruction to the midwives. The Fifth Word was carried from Herod to Bethlehem. One of the Lost Words dwelt among the Aztecs and hungered after their children.

Evil hides behind starched white masks. The ancient Aztec demon now conducts his affairs in the sterile environment of corporate medical abortion facilities. An insatiable hunger draws the demon to a sleepy Louisiana hamlet.

Monsignor, a mysterious priest of unknown age and origin, labors unseen to save the soul of a small town hidden deep within Louisiana's plantation country, nearly forgotten in a bend of the Mississippi River. *You'll be gripped from start to heart-stopping finish in this page-turning thriller.* With roots in Bram Stoker's Dracula, this horror novel reads like Stephen King's classic stories of towns being slowly devoured by an unseen evil and the people who unite against it. The book is set in southern Louisiana, an area the author brings to life with compelling detail based on his local knowledge.

THE CAJUN ZOMBIE CHRONICLES
THE CATHOLIC ZOMBIE APOCALYPSE!

THANKS FOR READING!

Totus Tuus

Made in the USA
Monee, IL
25 June 2024

60619477R00129